THE CELTIC CROSS

The New Celtic Library

Series Editor
Stuart Booth

•

The Celtic Tradition
David James

Celtic Saints
Dr. Bob Curran

The Celtic Cross
Nigel Pennick

Celtic Pilgrimages
Elaine Gill & Rev. David Everett

The Celtic Druids
Yowann Byghan

THE NEW CELTIC LIBRARY

THE CELTIC CROSS

Nigel Pennick

ST DAVID'S PRESS

Published in Wales in 2007 by St David's Press
an imprint of

Ashley Drake Publishing Ltd
PO Box 733
Cardiff
CF14 7ZY
www.ashleydrake.com

A CIP catalogue for this book is available from the British Library

ISBN 978 1 902719 18 4

Typeset by Mudra Typesetters

Printed in Malta by Gutenberg Press Limited

CONTENTS

AUTHOR'S NOTE: I use the terms BCE and CE to denote years 'Before the Common Era' and 'Common Era'. The terms BC (Before Christ) and AD (Anno Domini – the year of the Lord) are specifically Christian, while BCE and CE are ideologically neutral.

INTRODUCTION

The Celtic tradition is one of the most recognizable elements of contemporary European culture, and it is also one of the most ancient, able to trace its routes back over 2,700 years.

The Celts have always given great respect to the arts, especially the spoken word. In former times, the highest honours were bestowed upon the bards, and the druids taught their doctrines through the techniques of a highly developed art of memory. The Celtic worldview was non-literalistic: it was expressed through a complex series of symbols and metaphors that gave access to the invisible inner nature of things. Even when they were conquered, the Celts never lost their exceptional abilities.

The religion of the Celts was an integral part of the culture of everyday life, was nature-venerating, polytheistic, and recognized goddesses as well as gods, which were represented both aniconically and iconically. According to the best accounts, Pagan Celtic spirituality recognized the cyclic nature of existence, which involved reincarnation of individuals, and immediate continuity between the material world and the otherworld. The druidic teachings, which have come down to us through Welsh tradition, tell of an integrated relationship between humans and nature, expressed through a vast body of natural lore concerning the seasons, the stars, matter and existence. Celtic spirituality has always recognized that there is an unseen world that interpenetrates the visible world. Everything exists on several simultaneous levels: human consciousness interprets them as the physical, the spiritual and the symbolic. Celtic religion understood the course of nature as the will of the Gods. In accordance with this, they venerated both local and general deities, which they saw as being present in natural sanctuaries, especially in ensouled places in the landscape. So their main places of worship were at holy hills, springs, rivers, lakes, trees and in woodland. Thus, Celtic culture was integrated with nature, expressed through the multiple possibilities of life itself. Most of this traditional lore is still known and preserved in Celtic folk-tradition.

In such a context, the Celtic Cross is known throughout the world as the emblem of Celtic Christianity, and in many ways it can be considered the symbol of Celticness itself. In this book, I present an overview of the rich spiritual ground from which grew the Celtic Cross as we know it, celebrating its forerunners and the Celtic Cross itself through the diversity of historical designs and as a continuing manifestation of the living tradition of Celtic art.

Nigel Campbell Pennick
Cambridge, UK

Chapter 1

PRECEDENTS AND ORIGINS

In many ways, the Celtic Cross is a continuation and refinement of a number of aspects of traditional spiritual culture. Most fundamentally, it contains symbolic elements that express the relationship of human beings to the divine. These elements are transcendent of religious doctrine, belonging to the perennial philosophy which underlies all religions.

The Navel of the World

The concept of the navel of the world, now called by its Greek name, *omphalos*, was recognized as far back as ancient Egyptian times. The Egyptian world centre was more than a symbolic or theoretical place, for it was actually represented by an elliptical stone that marked the mid-point of the country.

Although it is primarily the navel of the world, there is a strong connection, not only linguistically, between the *omphalos* and the phallus. A number of *omphaloi* at other places were phallic in shape, and the Etruscans used phalloid stones as tomb-markers. In the Celtic realms, a comparable pillar-stone stood at Pfalzfeld in the Hunsrück, Germany, in the land once inhabited by the Treviri tribe. Surrounded by ropework, an Etruscan motif that later appears in Celtic crosses all over the British Isles, the carvings on this stone include a bearded human head with horns or a head-dress, surrounded by scrollwork in La Tène style. In Ireland, similar stone *omphaloi* have survived. The stone at Turoe in County Galway is an elliptical mark-stone that closely resembles the Delphic *omphalos* in shape and size, even down to the swirling patterns that spiral across its surface. Elsewhere in Ireland are stones that include a cushion-shaped *omphalos* at Castlestrange in County Roscommon and a stone at Mullaghmast in Kildare. The latter is the base of an ancient Pagan pillar. Another base of a round pillar, which, when intact, was probably approximately conical, exists at Killycluggan in County Cavan. These *omphalos*-pillars are the model from which the later designers of the Irish high crosses took their inspiration.

The concept of the stone that stands at the centre of the world, or, by association, the centre of a country or sacred area, was known else-where in northern Europe. Before the introduction of the Christian religion into western Norway, many sacred places possessed *Hellige hvide stene* (holy white stones). Many have been discovered beneath churches or old homesteads which in Pagan times served as places of worship. In Scotland, Clackmannan, a former inauguration-place of the Pictish kings, possesses a similar, but much larger, phallic megalith which stands by the church. Like other *omphaloi*, it hallows the centre-point of the land, where the spiritual essence is at its height. Such places were the natural spiritual centres of the priesthood, monarchs and lords. In England, the London Stone, recently refurbished, traditionally marks the centre and holds the 'luck' of the city of London, while the same function is ascribed to the Blue Stane of St Andrews in Scotland. In the Low Countries, the central points of town market-places, which in other places would be marked by a market cross, were marked by a blue stone. Thus, the tradition of the *omphalos* lives on as an integral element of modern cities.

Natural Phenomena

Another forerunner of the Celtic Cross can be seen in a striking natural phenomenon. Under certain weather conditions, sun-or moonlight shining through airborne ice crystals produces halo phenomena. These are more common in northern latitudes, and there are many recorded patterns of solar and lunar haloes, including arcs, circles and crosses, which have been exhaustively investigated by contemporary meteorologists. However, when one actually sees these events, they are most impressive, and no amount of scientific explanation can diminish their awesome effect upon the observer. Thus, in ancient times, they were seen as direct manifestations of the power of the solar and lunar deities. Most common among the many possible patterns is the sun-dog array, in which a parhelic spot of light or 'mock sun' appears on either side of the real sun, 22 degrees away from the sun's disc. Sometimes, from the 'mock suns' develops a circle that can produce a full sunwheel or even more complex patterns. The most important halo form in the present context is the sunwheel, which is a cross surrounded by a circle, with the actual sun at the centre and 'mock suns' at the four quarters. Also, according to many eye-witnesses over the years, spirit-lights that emanate from the earth sometimes take the form of an *omphalos*, a pillar, a *tau* or even a wheel-cross. St Trillo's seaside holy well chapel at Llandrillo-yn-Rhôs (Rhos-on-Sea) in north Wales was founded at a place where the saint saw a Celtic Cross of light emerge from the ground.

Quartered circles like this are common in Cretan artefacts from the Minoan period, and they are also known widely in Northern Europe in carvings dating from the Bronze Age. Among the many carvings, there are several variant forms of the wheel. The pattern that was adopted later by the Celtic Christian church, and taken to be the basic form, is the four-spoked wheel. Although it is by far the most common, however, it is not the only form, as the number of spokes are variable. There are also examples composed of two concentric circles. In the Scandinavian rock-carvings, these forms appear in the same contexts, and thus are assumed to be versions of one another rather than completely different symbols. The circles may be shown alone, or with appendages that can be interpreted as supports. Sometimes they are carried by human figures, either above the head or as shields. They are borne on ships, and depicted as the wheels of actual vehicles.

Some of the rock-carvings from Bohuslän in Sweden show figures that might be interpreted as the wheel symbol set up on some kind of support, such as a wooden or wickerwork framework. If this is the case, then the Celtic Cross has a direct precedent in the ceremonial symbolism of ancient northern-European solar Paganism.

The Wheel Symbol

As the means by which a vehicle travels, the wheel was a sacred object in its own right. In Pagan times, vehicles were buried frequently with their Celtic owners, perhaps to serve as the conveyance of the dead person in the otherworld. Both the sun and moon, worshipped as deities, were portrayed as driving chariots through the sky. In northern Europe, ritual vehicles were used to transport images of deities around the country in sacred journeys that sanctified or cleansed the land. Wagons accompanied the dead in La Tène period tumuli, the wheels being detached and ranged along the walls of the burial chamber. Even in Christian times, images of Jesus mounted on a wheeled donkey were pushed through the streets on Palm Sunday, perhaps in continuation of the rites of the wheel-god.

By themselves, wheels appear in Celtic Paganism as an attribute of the heavenly thunder-and-lightning god,

Taranis, 'The Thunderer', whom the Romans assimilated with Jupiter, and the British Christians with God the Father under the title Daronwy. The wheel-god Taranis was acknowledged by the Pagan Celts from the Balkans to the British Isles. Remains of the worship of the wheel-god have been found all over the Celtic realms. They range from coins, small wheel-brooches and votive images to lifesize statues of the deity. The shrine site at Cold Kitchen Hill in Wiltshire has yielded many wheel-form brooches and votive wheels. Sometimes, deities are portrayed with wheels. One is carved on the left side of a Roman altar dedicated to the Great God Jupiter, kept at Tullie House, Carlisle. A Gallo-Roman altar of Jupiter found at Laudun in Gard, France, shows the god holding a sceptre in his left hand, while on the right is an eagle and a five-spoked wheel. Another statue of Jupiter, found at Vaison in Vaucluse, France, shows the standing god holding a wheel, accompanied by an eagle.

Elsewhere, the wheel-god is depicted on the first-century BCE Celto-Thracian silver cauldron from Gundestrup in Denmark, while in medieval East Anglia the wheel-god became the hero-giant Tom Hickathrift, who saved the people of the Cambridgeshire Fens by defeating the fearsome giant of Wisbech. Hickathrift's weapons were not a sword and shield. Instead, he used the axle-tree of a cart as a quarterstaff, and a wheel as a shield.

In Huntingdonshire, a similar figure, called Old Hub, appeared alongside the molly dancers at the midsummer festivities, marking the high point of the sun in the year.

The wheel is the most significant attribute of the Celtic Cross, and it appeared in a pre-Christian context along with the columnar form on Roman columns dedicated to Jupiter. A different representation of the wheel-column can be seen on a pagan Roman grave-stela in Carlisle Museum. In the form of a rectangular slab surmounted by a triangular pediment containing a lunar crescent, it bears three wheel-crosses. One is at the apex of the pediment, while the other two are at the junction of the rectangle and the triangle. They are depicted as supported on bulbous pillars in the manner of Celtic Crosses. From this, it is possible that pillars with wheel-crosses existed in Roman times as Pagan, rather than Christian, monuments. In support of this hypothesis, there are Christian Anglo-Saxon representations of crosses which closely resemble their pre-Christian forerunners. The Lechmere stone at Hanley Castle, Hereford and Worcester, is a fine example of this type of cross.

In later iconography, the sunwheel was taken from the Pagan sun gods and goddesses and used as a symbol of the Christian godhead.

As a more abstract symbol, the sunwheel has continued to be a protective sigil until the present day. It was stamped by the Germanic Pagans on the funeral urns in which they buried the ashes of their dead. Also, as the *Circle of Columbkille,* the sunwheel cross was the talismanic sigil of St Columba. Celtic Christians used it to invoke his power as a protection against all harm. Sacred signs inscribed within a circle have a long history as magical talismans. Known generally as insigils, they play an important role in protection. Medieval Irish magicians ascribed great magical power to the circular design called Feisefin, the Wheel of Fionn MacCumhaill. Consisting of a circle on which certain letters are written in the ogham alphabet, Fionn's wheel was used as a protective talisman against harm from other human beings, or evil spirits. The Northern Tradition magic of Scandinavia and Britain uses similar insigils with bind-runes.

The Torc

The most characteristic artefact of Celtic culture is another round structure, the torc, which is literally a binding of metal. Originating in the fifth century BCE during the La Tène period, the torc is essentially a body ornament made of precious metal in the form of a curved rod with identical free ends that face one another, almost touching. In effect, torcs are incomplete circles. Worn on the neck or arm, they must be flexible enough to enable the wearer to put them on and take them off, but without damaging or breaking the metal. Torcs appear to have had a sacred meaning, for images of the gods show them wearing torcs around their necks, or holding them in their hands. Among the wealth of magnificent ancient Celtic artefacts, some of the most masterly craftsmanship is preserved in the torcs. The most remarkable collection of torcs comes from the splendid hoard found at Snettisham in Norfolk, England. Dating from the first century BCE, the treasure consists of golden torcs composed of exquisite ropework in metal. One of the more notable examples is in the form of a rope composed of eight strands, each strand of which is made of eight twisted golden rods. The fineness of detail and the regularity of the twined metal in these torcs is a demonstration of the highest skills possessed by the ancient Celtic goldsmiths. These wonderful ancient Celtic torcs are displayed in the British Museum.

While the curved bodies of torcs were composed of ornamented rods or ropework of precious metal, their terminals were fashioned into geometric forms or animal heads. A heavy silver torc from Trichtingen in southern Germany is a fine example. The Trichtingen torc has opposing terminals in the shape of bulls' heads, each of which wears a torc around his neck. There are literary references to Celtic torc terminals in the shape of dogs and other animals, as well as knob- and ring-shaped endings. The twisted ropework of the torc is an early example of the Celtic motif of the entwined or interlaced rope, which appears later in various ornamental and symbolic forms on Celtic Crosses. Like torcs, Iron Age Celtic chains are remarkable examples of the smith's craft where hard metal has been transformed into a flexible structure whose patterns prefigure the ornament on later Celtic Crosses.

The smiths who made them went far beyond mere utilitarian design, creating remarkable interweavings of skilfully patterned iron links. A related Celtic invention in the military field was chainmail, introduced around 300 BCE, and soon adopted by the Romans and other military powers. Like the torcs, chainmail shows the Celtic love of interpenetration of materials, in which individual rings of the hardest iron are interlocked to create an impenetrable, yet flexible, armour.

Roman Mosaics

The patterns of Roman mosaics are important forerunners of the designs used to adorn and embellish the much later Celtic Crosses. Basic crosses are present as patterns in the tesselation designs of early Roman mosaics in Britain.

Many Roman mosaics contain panels surrounded by the interlace pattern known as the guilloche chain, of which there are two basic types. One is usually composed of three 'ribbons' interlaced in the manner of much Celtic work. This form, which appears later throughout Celtic, Nordic and Romanesque art, was used universally in Roman mosaic. It was clearly an influence upon this kind of Celtic interlace pattern.

The wheel-cross actually appears in Roman mosaic work, as it does on tomb stelae. One fine example is in the mosaic of Orpheus found at Littlecote Park in Wiltshire. Dating from around the year 360, it has a wheel-cross roundel with an image of lyre-playing Orpheus at the centre. In the four quarters made by the cross are four goddesses, riding various beasts sidesaddle. They symbolize the four directions, the four elements and the four seasons.

Chapter 2

ARCHAIC CELTIC STONES

In the Hallstatt period, generally after 1000 BCE, the Celts lived in central Europe, for they had not yet migrated westwards and northwards to the British Isles. However, Celtic traditions there are recognizable as forerunners of what came later. In that period, the Celts set up aniconic stones as holy stopping-places in the landscape. In their form and location, they pre-figure the later Celtic Crosses. Many have a roughly humanoid form that continues the much older tradition of making stone representations of the female principle. Some of the central European stones, such as the Hallstatt period pillar-cross from Tübingen-Kilchberg in south Germany (now in the Württembergisches Landesmuseum in Stuttgart), have a 'head' part that is incised with an X-shape.

Dating from 1,000 years or more before the Christians adopted the cross, these stones resemble the much later Celtic stone crosses in parts of Cornwall and Wales. Even when the Celtic Cross had become a stylized form, certain sculptors made crosses that echo the shouldered humanoid forms of the earlier Continental stones. Surviving examples of this kind of 'goddess-cross' can be seen in west Wales at Carew and Nevern. A true goddess-stone like those on which the crosses are based still stands in its original position just outside the churchyard of St Martin's in Guernsey. She is La Gran'mère du Chimiquère, a Celtic goddess image which was revered there long before the church was built. In the form of a female Herm, 'The Grandmother of the Cemetery' is an armless stone figure with breasts and a radiate collar that resembles the patterns on some Celtic images in Germany.

A pointed stone with a rudimentary human face from Rottenburg, at Stammheim in Stuttgart, is an early type of humanoid stone. It is a megalith whose shape roughly suggested the human form, which was 'humanized' by having the suggestion of a face carved onto it. Later, actual human representations were carved by the Celts. Some appear to have been images of goddesses and gods, while others served as commemorative memorials to individuals. It is thought that the Celts took the idea of setting up memorial images of the deceased individual from the Etruscans. There was a similar tradition among the Pagan Slavs further east. They erected carved stone pillars in honour of deities such as Triglav, Svantovit and Gerovit. They were often square-section pillars with faces of the gods carved at the top. The Polish Husjatyn pillar, is a typical example. Its cap resembles the capstones on the Irish high crosses at Ahenny.

In addition to ancestral memorials, there were also representations of deities in animal form, for in European Paganism animals can be manifestations of the divine equally as well as the human form. Thus, in addition to goddesses and gods, the boar, deer, stag, horse, dog and wolf appear frequently in sacred art. Although animal attributes accompany many Celtic carvings of humanoid deities, they also appear by themselves on Gallic and Pictish memorials and in certain contexts on later Celtic Crosses. In addition to the spirits of the animal world, Celtic cosmology recognizes intermediate beings that exist somewhere between the human and the animal. They appear as human-animal form images that include serpent-footed and horned men.

Horns and the horn-like 'leaf-crown' surmount the human head in many La Tène carvings. These seem to pre-figure both the form of the wheel-head of crosses and the haloes surrounding the heads of saints and the deity in Christian iconography. This halo-like form appears in the hairstyles of Celtic goddesses such as Epona and The Mothers. Two-faced figures also appear in Pagan Celtic art. Usually called janiform, after the Roman god Janus, they seem to have originated in Etruscan practice.

Humanoid Celtic pillar-stones have also been discovered in the British Isles. The so-called serpent stone from Maryport, Cumbria, is a carved stone phallus with a human head at the top. A humanoid pillar-stone at Minnigaff in Dumfries and Galloway has a bearded human head at the top on one side, whle bearing a cross with a bird on the other. The head tops a pillar which has no other carving. Thus it resembles the *Herms* and *Xoana* that were characteristic monuments of European Paganism.

Pagan and Christian Images

In the early Christian period, the distinction between what constituted a Pagan and a Christian image was unclear. In every age, Celtic artists have juxtaposed suitable elements from different sources. They have never adopted images haphazardly, but always in an appropriate way that reinforced whatever archetype of primordial holiness was required by the spiritual scheme they sought to portray. Thus, on Celtic Crosses, we find representations that can be interpreted equally as representing different myths. So there is the image that can be interpreted as the archetype of the hunter, Daniel amid the lions, or the hero or god, such as Odin, who overcomes or else is devoured by the beasts. Many Celtic images that were made after Christianity was introduced show no discrimination between Pagan and Christian images. Rather, Pagan and Christian elements are juxtaposed in such a way that emphasizes their similarities rather than their differences. So, instead of bringing division, they reinforce the archetype of holiness that is represented by a specific character from the Christian canon. Thus, traditional Celtic sacred elements which originated in the Pagan La Tène era appear alongside images of Christian priests and themes from Christian mythology. They are a continual reminder that in the Celtic lands there was no break, but a gradual, seamless transition between Pagan and Christian culture.

However, images depicting specifically Christian subjects in Celtic art are different from Pagan ones. This is not because of any noticeable difference in artistic or stylistic treatment, but because without exception they illustrate episodes and themes from written Biblical texts. Although they also follow iconographical conventions, Pagan images illustrate an oral narrative of sacred stories. In general, Pagan images represent the pictorial language of myth, while Christian ones come from a literate structure. Thus, the Pagan images are nearer to folk art than are the Christian ones. While the church sought to edit the scriptures to produce a definitive text of the Christian stories and doctrines, in the Pagan, oral culture, there was no rigid narrative. Because the druids committed nothing to writing and relied on memory, there was no orthodoxy in the sense of 'religions of the book'. Oral myth lives in action, word and image, not in books. This is why it is often rather difficult to identify images of Pagan goddesses and gods, whose artistic attributes may be based upon oral traditions that are lost now, such as the episodes from the life of Loki on several Manx crosses.

A number of ancient Celtic churches contain some quite remarkable images within their fabric or churchyards. Close to the high cross at Cardonagh in Donegal is a stone pillar with an image of a priest with a bell. His form is similar to earlier Pagan images that exist *in situ* in Brittany, such as the twin images at Elven, Morbihan, called

Jean and Jeanne Babouin. Standing in a line inside the unroofed twelfth-century church on Boa Island in Lower Lough Erne, County Fermanagh, is a splendid collection of seven stone humanoid figures that date from around the year 900. They are both Pagan and Christian, including a *sheela-na-gig*, a seated man holding a book, an abbot or abbess with crozier and bell, and a squat figure in the cross-legged Celtic sitting position often associated with the antlered god Cernunnos. This figure has a large, horned, two-faced head. He appears again on a humanoid pillar-stone at Cardonagh, County Donegal, while a similar, squatting, antlered figure is present on the north cross at Clonmacnois.

At Rougham in County Clare stands another pillar-stone. This is in the form of a *tau* cross, the symbol of St Anthony of Egypt favoured by medieval stonemasons. It is carved with Celtic heads on the upper side. The churchyard of Caldragh has a two-faced janiform stone image which has a depression, perhaps for libations, between the heads. A curious stone preserved in the Margam Stones Museum in south Wales depicts an ithyphallic man. In his hands he holds two small phallus-shaped staves. Although the actual names and sometimes the meanings of these figures are forgotten in many places, the old Pagan deities are still remembered occasionally. One such instance is at Kirk Conchan, near Douglas on the Isle of Man, where there is a dog-headed image depicting the Manx Celtic god, Conchem, who has been assimilated with the Christian saint, Christopher. A number of stone crosses with dog carvings are known from this place.

The Celts were known for their cult of the human head, in which they decapitated their enemies and preserved their heads as sacred objects. The Celto-Ligurian shrines at Roqueperteuse and Entremont in Bouches-du-Rhône in the south of France are among the best documented of the Celtic head shrines. Because these sacred structures were destroyed in antiquity by the Romans, the cult skulls were preserved in the ruins. There, archaeologists discovered human heads placed in niches of the stone pillars that flanked the shrines. Stones with carved heads were also found at Entremont, and those that appear on later Celtic pillar-stones and stone crosses are representations of the real heads that once graced Celtic settlements. A Celtic head is integral with the head of the cross at Trevean in St Erth parish, Cornwall. According to ancient Celtic belief, the head contains the essence of the individual, and, by preserving the head, this part of the soul remains present after death. Although it is of Pagan origin, the Celtic cult of the head did not cease in Ireland or Scotland with the advent of Christianity. Until the seventeenth century, it remained the common practice to behead all of those slain or captured in battle. Also the heads of famous priests and monks were preserved as relics. Many Celtic churches contain human skulls still. The cult is recalled by the remarkable panel on Clonfert Cathedral, which demonstrates the Pythagorean number system known as the *tetraktys* by means of ten stone heads set in a triangular panel.

Tumulus Stones and *Leachta*

In Pagan times, it was customary to set up large memorial stones on top of the grave-mounds of the high and mighty. The ensemble of the burial mound with a standing stone or image on top of it is the forerunner of the Celtic high crosses, set upon their pyramidal or stepped bases. In Ireland, we can see other forerunners of the high crosses in the shape of the *leachta*. These are small rectangular drystone structures that resemble altars. On top of each *leacht* is a stone slab, often incised with crosses. Set into this is an upright stone cross, which is usually accompanied by large loose pebbles. These are used in votive rites of healing or cursing, being turned by the supplicants during prayers and invocations. The cross-slabs that stand on top of the *leachta* have much in common with the pillar-stones that stood on the Celtic burial-places in Pagan times. Furthermore, the Irish word *leacht* is derived from the Latin, *lectus*, meaning a bed, which is a name often gives to graves in Celtic countries. Naturally, because they are holy, no *leachta* have been excavated to see whether anyone is buried beneath them. Like crosses, *leachta* are holy stopping-places at which prayers are offered by devout people. Some sacred enclosures have a number of them, each of which has a slightly different character. For example, the island of Inishmurray in County Sligo has eleven *leachta*, which are used as stopping-places in ceremonial processions during religious festivals. It is likely that the erection of *leachta* was formerly widespread in Celtic countries, and that the enormous calvaries of Brittany that were erected much later are a development of them.

The custom of erecting a memorial stone on top of a burial mound was widespread in ancient European Paganism. Many such Celtic mounds have been excavated, and we are fortunate that modern archaeology has recovered the splendour of some of the burials that lay beneath the mounds. The exquisite artefacts excavated from the burials represent themes recorded later in the Celtic spiritual literature of Ireland and Britain. They recall the ensouled world of Celtic tradition, in which every artefact is not merely an object but possesses its own unique personality.

Each thing, made a by a Celtic craftsperson specially according to spiritual principles, contains within itself multiple meanings. The interchangeable forms of Celtic art express the plurality of existence, the multifaceted experiences of life, death and rebirth. Each type of artefact reflects its own symbolic qualities and mythic traditions which to this day continue to inspire contemporary Celtic art and spirituality. On both memorial stones and crosses, the patterns of Celtic art fade imperceptibly from one form into another, yet they always retain the same essence. Each Celtic artefact, from the largest stone to the smallest coin, expresses different aspects of this essential continuity, in which the forms of this material world and the otherworldly realm of spirit interpenetrate one another. According to the Celtic worldview, the realms of animals and humans, goddesses and gods, life and death are not separate. They are aspects of a great integrated continuum, in which everything is an aspect of the whole. According to the ancient maxim, 'as above, so below', in the Celtic worldview the structure of the greater world is reflected in the lesser. This is expressed in Celtic art, whose principles reflect the basic way that nature is structured. Each carved piece of wood or stone, each torc, ring and metal fitment, however small, is a perfect instance of this principle, which was not destroyed when the Christian religion was introduced, but was nurtured and developed. Thus, the spirit of Celtic art was maintained within the Celtic church, and continued to underpin the newer Celtic culture without compromising its fundamental principles.

Chapter 3

THE SIGNS OF THE LAND

Tattooing is an ancient means of permanently identifying oneself. Its origins are lost in antiquity, but it has been used in Europe for over 5,000 years. 'Ötzi', a man found frozen in the Austrian Alps in 1991, and dating from around 3300 BCE, had a cross tattooed on his left knee and other signs composed of dots and lines elsewhere. According to Herodotus, in the fifth century BCE the brave and renowned Scythian warriors were tattooed, and their tombs at Bashadar, Pazyryk, Shibe and Tuekta in the High Altai region of Siberia have yielded embalmed and frozen bodies preserved well enough to show what these tattoos were like. Known Scythian tattoo motifs include beaked horses, rams, lions, fish and plants. Many Scythian beasts are depicted with spirals at the joints in the manner of the later Celtic animal artwork. There are historic links between the Celts and the Scythians, and Scythian elements appear in the early Celtic art of the La Tène period. During the same period, aristocratic Thracian women were being tattooed. Thracian priestesses of Dionysos are shown with their tattoos on fifth-century BCE Greek vases. Later, the sword-wielding woman attacking the bull on the base of the Celtic-influenced Gundestrup Cauldron (first century BCE) is depicted with tattoos similar to those of Thracian priestesses. In the first century BCE, Julius Caesar reported that the Britons painted themselves with blue woad, and this may refer to tattoos as well as war-paint. The Lindow Man, whose body was preserved in a bog, was tattooed, and the Picts were famed for the tattoos that they wore. Writing around the year 600, Isidore of Seville tells that the Picts were so called because their bodies were covered with pictures pricked into their skin using needles and coloured with herbs. The Celtic warriors' custom of fighting naked may in part have been intended to show off their body tattoos which served both to identify the warrior and to demonstrate his exploits.

We may have an idea of what Celtic tattoos looked like. Celtic coins found in the Channel Islands show that some Celts wore tattoos on the cheeks. The face of the sun god or Gorgo that once graced the pediment of the Celto-Roman temple at Bath has lines that may reproduce tattoos. The Celtic custom of depicting symbols of the gods on the body is recorded in the histories of St Kentigern. In his mission to the Cumbrians in what is now Scotland, St Kentigern condemned those people who 'disfigured' their faces and bodies with tattoos in honour of the Pagan gods. Kentigern was following an edict of the Emperor Constantine (287–337), who forbade tattoos as a disfigurement of God's image in the human form.

Contemporary Irish churchmen, too, considered tattoos to be symbols or badges of Paganism, as opposed to the tonsure of Christian monks. Later, in the year 785, the Synod of Calcuth condemned the practice as un-Christian. The *Book of Kells*, written shortly afterwards, shows human figures with interlace, circle and point patterns on the body.

To the Pagan Celts, the multivalent deities could be symbolized both by aniconic and iconic images and by animals that embodied their character and power. Each of these animals was emblematical of the tribe, being also a manifestation in animal form of the tribal goddess or god.

Thus, it is quite possible that Pictish symbol-stones reproduce the tattoos that were on the body of the person whom they commemorated. It is clear that the Christian church made a successful attempt to suppress the practice of tattooing, because it was Pagan. The Pictish king became Christian in the year 710. Then, cross-slabs began to supersede the earlier picture-stones and the Pictish symbols were subordinated to the cross, finally being relegated to the back of the stones. As the practice of tattooing died out, and Latin writing was introduced, perhaps there was no longer the need or indeed the possibility to identify an individual by his or her tattoos.

However, individual signs did not die out. Though their Pagan connections may have faded, they have continued until the present as the totems and heraldic devices of clans and families. The tattoos that people wore on their bodies, their tribal, clan and family emblems, colours and heraldry are linked intimately to the landscape from which they come. They are as much a part of the land as the rivers and hills, fields and trackways, villages and holy places that make up the traditional landscape of northern Europe.

Standing stones and stone crosses do not exist separately from the landscape in which they stand. They are important landmarks in their own right, often bearing their own names which tell something of their history and meaning. Thus, stones and crosses are repositories of the local spirit of place, preserving and expressing the particular character of the land of which they are part. Crosses are always stopping-places in the landscape, places on pathways where travellers can rest, pray and restore body and spirit before going on their way. In difficult terrain, crosses mark the way, showing the wayfarer the most favourable path between villages or monasteries.

Naming the Land

In early days of Christianity, it was customary for missionaries to set up preaching-stations at stopping-places on trackways, in markets or at other locations where people passed by or gathered together. These holy stopping-places where the priest offered prayers and preached the gospel were marked by a standing cross. This could be either a portable processional staff-cross temporarily put into the ground during sacred activities, and removed afterwards, in the manner of a maypole, or a permanent cross of some kind. When the missionary priest died, his followers would bury him at one of these stopping-places, creating further layers of sanctity upon an already hallowed place. Such standing crosses were used for outdoor services in places where there was no church. In the sixth century, the Roman Emperor Justinian ordered that the erection of a cross should precede the building of a church, and the consecration ceremony for churchyards involved the erection of a wooden cross on the boundary at each of the four cardinal directions. A cross could serve as a place of worship where there was no church, as recorded in 'The Life of St Willibald' (*The Lives of the British Saints*, 1908), which tells that Saxon land-owners erected crosses at which daily worship was held, in preference to far more expensive churches.

Pilgrimage, the spiritual journey in which the devotee travels in a prayerful, meditative way to a holy place, has always played an important part in religion. Although making a pilgrimage to the Holy Land or Rome was considered good for Christian souls, in practical terms this was rarely possible. As an inferior substitute for the real thing, local pilgrimages and sacred circuits or 'rounds' were undertaken. Walking prayerfully around a relatively small area, the pilgrim visited a number of holy places in a certain order. These places were often marked by crosses. Whether a sacred circuit was around a churchyard, through a town, or around a whole parish, it would take only a day at most to complete. Visiting each cross or other holy stopping-place in turn, the pilgrim said appropriate prayers and offered oblations at each one. Today, sometimes, rounds are undertaken on the local saint's day. In Britanny, this ceremony is known as a Pardon, while in Ireland it is called the saint's Pattern or Patron. At such events, pilgrims experience a progressive heightening of their religious experience through the medium of the geomythic landscape.

In England, the holy stopping-places on the monastic trackway across Dartmoor between Tavistock Abbey and Buckfast Abbey in Devon are marked by a particularly well-preserved series of named crosses that serve as waymarkers and spiritual support for the wayfarer.

In East Anglia, crosses waymarked the pilgrimage routes to the shrine of Our Lady at Walsingham, one of the major shrines of medieval Britain.

Another series of crosses is associated with Aldhelm of Malmesbury, who died in the year 709. The Wiltshire monastery of Malmesbury was founded by Maeldubh, an Irishman, and Celtic traditions prevailed there under the rule of the West Saxons. According to legend, St Aldhelm was born in a churchyard at the foot of a standing cross, becoming in due course a noted prelate of the church. After a long life of founding new churches and doubtless setting up crosses, Aldhelm died at Doulting in the house of his Pagan friend, Kenred. His body was borne back to Malmesbury in solemn procession from Doulting. The cortège took a circuitous ceremonial route which involved seven stages of seven miles a day. Later, stone crosses were erected at the stopping-places where the cortège had halted. Fragments of cross at Bath Abbey, Colerne and Littleton Drew are said to be their remnants.

In Celtic tradition, there is no hard-and-fast rule that divides mythology from history. Although they are frequently dismissed as having originated in attempts by primitive poets to explain the unknown, myths nevertheless contain primordial truths. They are not intended to be taken literally, for they exist outside physical reality in the realm of metaphor. In order to understand their inner nature, we must take these myths on their own terms, neither dismissing them as meaningless fantasies nor rationalizing them. It is possible to interpret any landscape myth in a number of different ways, each of which may prove insightful. Essentially, our approach to such myths and legends is individual and personal. Throughout the sacred landscape of the British Isles and Brittany, the names of crosses, and the stories told about them, weave a geomythic fabric of the land which expresses its character in a particular way. So, in Brittany, the cross at the place called La Croix des Sept Chemins, where seven roads meet, marks the spot where seven brothers (Connec, Dardanaou, Gerna, Gonery, Jort, Merhé and Quidec) embraced and left to preach the gospel. All of them became saints in the Celtic church, for each founded a chapel in the direction in which he went. Through the Celtic Cross, following on from the earlier Pagan stone, ancestral heritage is maintained and the mythic spirit of the landscape lives through those who experience it.

Celtic tradition celebrates multiplicity. Its mythology is full of events that take place at a certain place through the coming-together of a number of unrelated causes, each of which could cause the event alone. Integrating unrelated things into a coherent whole is one of the arts of the Celtic bard. The Irish wizard Bec mac Dé is reputed to have been able to hear nine separate questions from nine different people at one time, and to respond to them with a single answer. Similarly, the Celtic Cross, with its origins in many different sacred areas, is the point of coincidence that reflects the Celtic principle of unity in multiplicity.

In traditional Celtic society, there was nothing impersonal. Each thing that a man or woman encountered in everyday living had its own life, too. Each thing was a subject, not an object, which could be spoken of by its own, personal, name. This was because every natural thing, human artefact and part of the landscape was named. Each name reflected some inner nature, a personal quality that had meaning. In the ensouled Celtic worldview, the personality of every place and artefact was recognized to be as real as the individual personalities of human beings. This is the case with seemingly inanimate objects such as stones and crosses. Such an ensouled world can only exist when there is intimate personal contact with existence. When individual things are made by craftspeople, then no two are the same, but once manufacturing industry arose, with mass-production of multiple things, then the personal contact was lost. Artefacts became anonymous products, whose essential character no longer originated in the individual character of its maker and users. Today, many of the names of the landscape are lost or forgotten, or overlain by meaningless inventions. The naming of the world has continued in a few specialized areas, such as in the names of private and public houses, hotels, aircraft and ships. On a smaller level, it is even less frequent, with the occasional exception of particularly personal possessions such as cars, knives, guns and guitars.

Chapter 4

HEAVENLY COLUMNS

The Celtic Cross has a number of antecedents, all of which have contributed their particular qualities. Places where paths and trackways join, especially crossroads, are marked in every culture as special spiritual places somehow different from the rest of the world. According to cosmic symbolism, the crossroads is the place where the cosmic axis between the underworld and the upperworld intersects with middle earth. Spiritually, the crossroads is a place where the distinction between the physical plane and the non-material worlds is less certain. In ancient Greece and Rome, crossroads were marked with an ithyphallic pillar-image of Hermes (Mercury), god of the crossways and psychopomp of the dead. Known as a *Herm*, frequently the pillar was sheltered by a tree and accompanied by an altar upon which travellers made offerings.

Crossroads were significant places in ancient Celtic culture. In his account of the Gauls, Julius Caesar stated that the chief god of the Celts was: 'Mercury, of whom there are many images throughout Gaul: he is considered to be the originator of all of the arts; the god who indicates the right road and guides the traveller's footsteps; he is the great patron of trade and riches.' The god about whom Caesar wrote has the attributes of the Irish god Lugh. In places influenced by Germanic and Scandinavian Paganism, the crossroads was a holy place of the god of commerce and interchange, Woden, who was also the god of hanged men.

Thus, in the north, the crossroads were especially sacred to the dead, being a place where, at certain times, it was possible to commune with departed spirits. When the Christian religion was introduced, the sacred cross of roads was re-interpreted naturally as being symbolic of the cross of Christ, at which priests erected stone crosses that served as stopping-places for wayfarers and pilgrims.

The Maypole

The general principle of the heavenly column appears to be very ancient, seemingly going back at least 3,000 years. A remarkable pointed conical golden object called a *goldkegel* found at Ezelsdorf, near Nuremberg, and dating from 1100 BCE, is believed to be the top of such a pillar. Also, from the evidence of enormous post-holes, it appears that votive posts were erected in the Celtic sacred enclosures favoured in Germany and France. In former times, the Welsh maypole was a birch tree, as it is in some parts of Germany today. In his *Crefydd yr Oesoedd Tywyll* (1852), the bard Nefydd (William Roberts) left an account of Welsh traditions of *Codi'r Fedwen* (raising the birch), which was accompanied by the *dawns y fedwen* (the dance of the birch), a kind of morris dancing. In more recent times, maypoles have been set up each year to celebrate the Celtic festival of Beltane. The custom was formerly widespread throughout northern Europe, but its use has dwindled in the British Isles. We know of the customs from relatively recent records, but there is no reason to suggest that they were not substantially the same in ancient times. Indeed, during the Reformation, Protestants pointed out their Pagan origin and condemned them as such, and that was the end of the Maytide celebrations in many places.

Jupiter Columns

Another forerunner of the Celtic cross is the Jupiter Column, a type of monument that, came into being as the result of a remarkable incident. In 65 BCE, the image of Jupiter at the Capitol in Rome was destroyed by a lightning strike, along with stone tablets of the law and a statue of one of the twins beneath the Roman wolf. The destruction of some of the most sacred images of Rome was recognized as a disastrous omen for Roman society and the future of the city.

Whether the original, destroyed image of Jupiter had been set upon a column is uncertain; but, after Etruscan *haruspices* had investigated the omens, the augurs decided to set up a column to Jupiter on the site of the previous image. This was erected ceremonially in 63 BCE, with an image of the god watching over his people. To the Romans, Jupiter, father of the gods and the people, was the great architect of the universe, sustainer of all. The architectural column is thus completely appropriate as a symbol of the god. As protector of the city, the new column became the model for others in the western Roman Empire. Outside Italy, Jupiter Columns are found in the Celtic realms that came under Roman rule. While they are known from Britain, Brittany and most of France, the vast majority of columns have been discovered in Lorraine and Alsace and the Rhineland region of Germany.

Symbolically, Jupiter Columns are a summation of time and space, and the Roman pantheon. Later, when Christianity superseded Paganism as the state religion, this scheme of portraying the gods and goddesses on a column was taken up and interpreted according to the newer doctrines. The Celtic Crosses that bear images of the figures of the three-fold godhead, prophets, patriarchs and saints are a re-interpretation of the scheme of the Jupiter Columns. The classical column was too good a symbolic form to abandon.

Chapter 5

EARLY CELTIC CROSSES

The Celtic Cross did not evolve out of nothing, or even as the development of a single precursor. As we have seen, it is a syncretic structure that came into being under a particular set of conditions as the result of an accumulation of ideas, symbols and traditions. In its most basic form, the cross itself was not originally Christian, nor was it used openly in the earliest years of the Christian religion. Before it was adopted as an exclusively Christian sign in the year 680, the cross was a symbol of land-measure, employed by diviners and the *agrimensores*, members of the Roman guild of surveyors. In his *De Divinatione*, Cicero, who was an augur, tells that in his time the staff carried by the Roman augurs was in the form of a cross. As time passed, however, the generally sacred symbol of the cross gradually developed a more specific, Christian meaning.

Images close to the later Celtic Cross existed in the Coptic church. A good example can be seen in the Coptic manuscript known as the *Codex Brucianus*. Preserved in the Bodleian Library at Oxford, it has an illuminated cover in the form of an ornamented ankh-cross. In Egyptian religious iconography, the ankh or *crux ansata* was the symbol for life. The Coptic Christians took the symbol and amalgamated it with the wheel and cross. The Coptic funerary stela from Armant near Luxor shows how they integrated the older Egyptian symbols for life with the newer Christian ones. Interestingly, the scribe of the *Codex Brucianus* has illuminated the ankh-cross with interlace patterns and tesselations that today are the epitome of the Celtic Cross.

The Sign of the Cross

Like the ankh before it, the cross was invested with great power both to consecrate and to ward off harm. Writing in his *De Corona Militis*, at the end of the second century, Tertullian tells how the early Christians used the cross as a universal protective gesture: 'At every commencement of business, whenever we go in or come out of any place, when we dress for a journey, when we go into a bath, when we go to meat, when lights are brought in, when we lie down or sit down, and whatever business we have, we make on our foreheads the sign of the cross.' When the Christians of that time wanted to signify Christ, however, they used symbols other than the cross. Most popular were the fish, the lamb, the good shepherd (taken from images of Apollo), the Greek letters *alpha* and *omega*, and the *chi-rho* monogram. This latter sign took a number of forms, the earliest of which was made with the Greek letters *X* (*chi*) and *P* (*rho*) as on the Coptic stela. Sometimes, the monogram was shown inside a circle or laurel wreath. In Britain, this earliest form of *chi-rho* exists in the floor mosaic from the Roman house at Hinton St Mary in Dorset, preserved in the British Museum.

By the late fourth century, there was the tendency to turn the *X* into an upright position, thereby converting the *chi-rho* into a looped-headed vertical cross. A good example of this type of *chi-rho* can be seen on a stone which is preserved inside the church at Penmachno in Gwynedd. Bearing a Latin inscription that reads (in translation) 'Carausius lies here in this cairn', the stone, which stood on a burialcairn in continuation of Celtic Pagan tradition, has been dated to the late fifth or early sixth century. Above the inscription is a looped cross *chi-rho* without a surrounding circle. Around the late fifth century, Celtic carvers began to make sunwheel crosses with a right-facing hook in the upper arm. Finally, the hook or *P* was dropped, and a cross in a circle was the result. Sometimes it was accompanied by the Greek letters *alpha* and *omega*, symbolizing the beginning and the end. A pillar-stone preserved in the chapel at Kirkmadrine in Galloway is a good example of such a hooked-head cross within a circle. It was not until the year 680 that the cross and related crucifix was adopted officially by the church at a General Council held in Constantinople, when at last a standardized form was agreed for Christian use.

An early cross-stone in the Carmarthen Museum collection is a stone taken from Castelldwyran in Dyfed, called 'The Memorial of Voteporix Protector'. It is a pointed megalith with inscriptions in Latin and ogham. Prominent above the inscription is a ring-cross or sunwheel without any hook or P on the top arm. It is a characteristic form, for similar inscribed stones were erected in other parts of the British Isles at this time. In Ireland, there are numerous extant slabs carved with wheel-crosses composed of geometrically drawn arcs. Although most of the arc-crosses have four arms, this number is not fixed. Some have six or seven arms. Perhaps these are not Christian monuments at all, but memorials of Pagans or those of dual faith. However, multiple-armed wheels appear on stones that are certainly Christian. A notable cross-slab at Maughold on the Isle of Man, dating from the late seventh or early eighth century, has as its main carving not a cross but a six-fold consecration-wheel of the kind common on Roman Pagan altars and associated with the goddess Juno. However, its Christian intent is without question, for the six-fold wheel is surrounded by an inscription dedicated to the bishop Irneit, carved in a circle in the manner of seals. Beneath it are two Latin crosses accompanied by texts.

Although they are rare, certain Irish stones of this type survive because they are stopping-places on pilgrimage routes set up by early missionaries. In the valley of Glencolmkille in County Donegal is a series of cross-carved stones, set up on cairns at which present-day pilgrims pray like their forebears did. Other stones of this type mark the tracks to and on Mount Brandon, around Croagh Patrick, on Caher Island and at the pilgrimage centres of Ballyvourney, Clonmacnois and Glendalough. They can also be found outside Ireland, in Iona and the Shetland Isles.

Megalithic Cross-Slabs and Holed Stones

The cross-slab at the former monastery of Reask in County Kerry is of interest as a surviving bridge between the older and the newer forms of Celtic art. The carvings on the cross at Reask are comparable with patterns on Pagan stones from the La Tène Celtic culture in what is now south Germany. The Reask stone is irregular in shape, and the fourfold cross pattern cut into it has been squashed from a true circle to fit the asymmetrical megalith upon which it is carved. However, it is clear that there is a reason for this beyond laziness or incompetence. When one views the cross from a distance, it is apparent that the shape of its top imitates that of the distant horizon. This reflectivity of stone profile and horizon can be seen elsewhere in the British Isles. Some stone circles, most notably at Castlerigg in Cumbria, have this feature in almost every megalith. The Reask stone is clearly within this megalithic tradition. In addition to its horizon-following shape, it was also once pierced by a hole like many ancient magical megaliths, but this is now broken out. The practice of drilling holes through stones is archaic, and many ancient rockfaces and megaliths contain 'cup-marks' where people have made shallow depressions in the stone. Cup-marks are especially prevalent on sculpted stones such as those at Newgrange and other megalithic holy places. Although it cannot be stated for certain why the ancient cup-marks were made, more recent folk-tradition shows that it was customary to scrape away dust from holy stones for use as a medicinal remedy.

Cup-marks are found on stones in the fabric of churches and crosses as well as upon archaic megaliths. A number of Cornish cross-shafts are covered with drilled-out holes, such as that in the old churchyard of Merthyr Uny, in the parish of St Wendron. Other Cornish crosses have a depression at the centre of the wheel-head where a boss might be. Crosses like this exist or have existed at Bodmin, Callyworth, Crowan, Clowance, Lanteglos and St Kew. In addition to these depressions, a number of extant Celtic stones have holes drilled right through them. These holes have a function in folk-magic and spiritual development, being used for the promotion of fertility, healing and seership. Some holed stones are pilgrims' stations visited during saints' Patterns. Each has its own particular custom associated with it, such as looking through the hole, passing something, or holding hands through it. There is a hole in the top of an ogham-inscribed pillar-stone that stands at a stopping-place on the Saint's Road at Kilmakedar on the Dingle Peninsula. At Glencolmkille, a stone slab marking the stopping-place called Farranmacbride has a hole at the centre of the wheel-cross near the top. It is said that the pilgrim who looks through the hole while 'doing the round' will get a glimpse of heaven.

The Pictish cross-slab at Aberlemno has one of the four round corners of the cross drilled right through, and many wheel-headed crosses have not one hole, but four, that connect the front with the back. More generally, the whole genre of 'four-holed' and wheel-headed crosses are instances of the veneration of holy holed stones. The motif of the four holes, present already in German Celtic stones from the sixth century BCE, appears also in the early pillar-cross from Carn Caca at Melin-cwrt, Resolfen, in West Glamorgan. This has a carved circle in which is a cross potent. This kind of cross is composed of four T-shaped pieces, which alludes to the *tau* cross, symbol of the father of monasticism, St Anthony of Egypt. In the four angles of this cross are four depressions or dots that appear in later crosses as holes or circles.

Some of these standing cross-stones are likely to have been holy stones sacred to the elder faith that were reconsecrated as Christian monuments by being carved with the symbols of the newer religion. 'The earliest preachers of Christianity do not seem to have made violent attacks upon the creeds and beliefs of their converts,' wrote Alfred Rimmer in *Ancient Stone Crosses of England* (Virtue and Co, 1875), '... they pointed to the groves and holy wells, and dedicated them in another name. Crossroads also were held peculiarly sacred in the early times, and even as far back as the period of the Druids they were marked by upright stones, not dissimilar to those we see at Stonehenge, though, of course, much smaller, and these stones were chiselled on the upper part with a cross in relief.' Although many Celtic churches were founded on new sites, some took over places of Pagan sanctity. The standing stones that marked the old sanctuaries were re-used in the fabric of the new building, or allowed to remain in the churchyard re-consecrated as crosses. There are many instances of this process throughout the Celtic realms. In Scotland, the Fifeshire church of Dunino incorporates megaliths which were Christianized with crosses inscribed upon them. An example of a standing stone that became a kind of cross can be seen in the churchyard at Bridell in Dyfed, which contains a megalith upon which is an ogham inscription commemorating 'Nettasagrus, descendant of Brecos'. A cross inscribed inside a circle was added later. In Wales, the re-use of ancient stones was a common practice throughout history, continuing well into the nineteenth century. In 1876, for instance, an ogham-inscribed wheel-cross slab at Staynton in Pembrokeshire was re-used as the tombstone of T. Harries, who died on 30 January that year, aged 84.

Re-consecrated Stones

Re-dedication of megaliths by churchmen is recorded in ancient accounts of the acts of early Celtic priests and monks. Brittany contains many standing stones that have been made into Christian monuments by having a cross carved upon them. There are probably more in that region than anywhere else in western Europe; but it was commonplace throughout the Celtic realms. In his 'The Acts of Patrick' in *The Book of Armagh*, Tirechan describes how St Patrick carved a cross on a rock at Lia na Manach near the church of Kilmore in County Mayo. The Welsh saint, Samson, seems to have been one of the most active re-dedicators. The 'Life of St Samson' (*The Lives of the British Saints*, Honourable Society of Cymmrodorion, 1908) recounts that when the early sixth-century saint was passing through Cornwall on his way from Wales to Brittany he travelled through a region called Tricurius. There he encountered some people performing ceremonies at what the chronicler calls an 'abominable image', that is, a standing stone. Unlike his Biblical namesake, who toppled the pillars of the Philistines, this Samson did not fell the stone, but re-dedicated it to Christian use by cutting a cross upon it. Although the exact place that this occurred is not identified, there are several possible locations.

In Glamorgan, south Wales, are the standing stones called *Ffust Samson* (Samson's flail), Samson's Jack and *Carreg Samson* (Samson's stone). Elsewhere in Wales are other stones called *Carreg Samson*. The name is given to a standing stone on the mountainside at Llandewi Brefi, a stone cross near the church porch at Llanbadarn Fawr near Aberystwyth, and two cromlechs in north Pembrokeshire, Dyfed. Also in this area are stones called *Marbl Samson* (Samson's marble) and *Bys Samson* (Samson's finger). Samson's stones in south Wales stand on the route of his journey from Llantwit Major to Dôl in Brittany, and, not surprisingly, there are St Samson's stones in Brittany, too. A menhir at Mont-Dôl, Ile-et-Vilaine, is called St Samson's Mitre, and at Penvern, Côte-du-Nord, is another menhir named after the saint. Next to it stands a chapel dedicated to Samson, which was constructed between 1575 and 1631.

In Wales, the megalith sacred to another early Celtic missionary, St Beuno, still stands at Berriew in Powys, in the shape of Beuno's Stone. The animal-related rites conducted until the last century at Beuno's shrine, at Clynnog Fawr in the Lleyn, were the direct continuation of Celtic Paganism. It seems that, like many priests of the Celtic church, Beuno took over the shrines of the elder faith for Christian use while altering their ceremonial character very little. Elsewhere, other Celtic priests, whose names are not recorded, also appropriated the holy stones of the elder faith. At Llanfaelog in Anglesey, a prehistoric cup-marked menhir was re-dedicated by having a cross cut upon it, while at East Worlington in Devon is the megalith called the Long Stone, which bears no fewer than five incised crosses.

Some Cornish antiquaries have considered a number of the more archaic-looking stone crosses in that county to be of druidic, rather than Christian origin. In their form, they appear close to continental stones of the Hallstatt period, such as the Kilchberg stone in south Germany. Thus it is possible that at least some of the Cornish crosses are stones of the elder faith, re-consecrated for Christian use. 'The early pillar "crosses", though accounted Christian when tested by inscription and decoration,' wrote Walter Johnson in 1912 in his *Byways in Archaeology*, 'may yet have an earlier origin ... many of the crosses and calvaries of Brittany, "with shapeless sculpture decked", are merely primitive menhirs adapted by the Christian artificer, and anyone who, like the writer, has had the opportunity of comparing the Breton sites with the kindred group of our English Brittany, will readily agree that a similar story may be told of Cornwall.'

Although it ceased in the early middle ages in Britain, when people began to destroy standing stones, the alteration of megaliths into Christian monuments continued in France until shortly before the Revolution. A re-dedicated menhir at Dôl (Ile-et-Vilaine), bears a metal cross on top of the 9.5 metre (30 ft) stone, while the Dolmen de la Belle Vue at Carnac has a stone cross set upon it. In 1826, Sir Richard Colt Hoare published an engraving of this cross under the title of 'Triumph of Christianity over Druidism'. The process of converting megaliths into crosses was associated usually with some specific local religious activity. For instance, in 1674, in connection with the construction of a new chapel nearby, a prehistoric megalith at Penvern in Brittany was re-dedicated by a Christian priest. This involved cutting down its summit to make a cross, and carving Christian emblems upon the remaining body of the stone. At Rungleo in Finistère is the Croix des Douze Apôtres. This is another megalith upon which Christian figures have been carved. At Pleumeur-Bodou in the Côtes-du-Nord is one which in the eighteenth century was cut with the cross and symbols of Christ's passion.

The last-known conversion of a megalith in France occurred in Alsace in 1787, when a megalith near Althorn known as the Breitenstein was re-carved as the result of a fulfilled vow. Thus, the Breitenstein became another 'Twelve Apostles Stone'. Not all Celtic Crosses in France are altered megaliths, however. Ancient crosses similar to those in Cornwall and the Isles of Scilly exist in several Breton churchyards. The crosses are of both the wheel-head and plain form. The churchyard at Ploudalmezou has a notable wheel-head cross on a stepped base. It is dedicated to St Pol de Léon, as are the other crosses there. The holy well of Saint-Cado is topped by a fine Celtic cross with a crucifixion at the centre reminiscent of that on the Cross of the Scriptures at Clonmacnois.

Chapter 6

EVOLUTION OF THE CELTIC CROSS

At the end of the fourth century, the mission of St Ninian to the people who lived north of the Roman province of Britain led to the foundation of the first Christian church in Caledonia. This was the so-called *Candida Casa* (White House) at Whithorn in Galloway. In the fifth and sixth centuries, the *Candida Casa* was a centre of Christian missionary activity in northern Britain and Ireland. St Enda, founder of the early monastery at Killeany on the Aran island of Inishmore, was an alumnus of Whithorn. There are few remains of Ninian's church, but a number of early Christian tomb-slabs at Whithorn and Kirkmadrine. The oldest Christian monument known from Scotland was discovered close to the site of Ninian's *Candida Casa*. It is an early fifth-century stone carved with a Latin inscription commemorating Latinus, his daughter and his grandson, Barrovadus, who set up the monument. At Kirkmadrine are three more memorial stones with Latin inscriptions and the *chi-rho* monogram. The associated holy place of Physgyll, St Ninian's Cave, on the foreshore about 5 km (3 miles) from Whithorn, has a number of early memorial crosses, some carved in the living rock, and some on separate stones.

Memorials and Cross-Slabs

Most Welsh memorial stones dating from the fifth to the seventh century are megaliths, unworked stones whose natural shapes were appropriate for inscriptions to be carved on them with the minimum of effort. Like the earlier megaliths, they were intended to stand upright as memorials that marked the burial places of important people, or sometimes the boundaries between territories. The earliest inscriptions are in Roman capitals, recalling that it was only a few years since Britain was a province of the Roman Empire. Later, however, as the memory of being Roman faded, this changed, and half-uncials, a character-type taken from Christian manuscripts, were used instead.

It appears to have been customary among the Pagan Anglo-Saxons who did not cremate their dead to bury a runestone with the body. Around the seventh century, stonecarvers began to incise crosses upon similar stones, some of which were intended to lie flat above the dead person, and not to stand up as a tombstone. Northumbrian 'pillow-stones' are known from the monastic cemeteries of Hartlepool and Lindisfarne, and a few other places including Billingham and Birtley in County Durham. Their name is misleading, for they were not placed beneath the head of the corpse, but over the face or on the chest. Closely related to Irish slabs, of which the largest collection can be seen at Clonmacnois, the Northumbrian pillow-stones are rectangular, with an incised cross-pattern. In Merovingian France at this time, it was becoming fashionable to mark Christian burials by flat slabs carved with ring-crosses.

Related to the Celtic wheel-head is the type of flat slab which has a cross at each end. These end-crosses are connected by a bar that forms another cross at the centre dividing the field into four panels, inside which is ornament. Early examples of this type exist at Sockburn in County Durham and Spennithorne in North Yorkshire. The majority of known slabs of this kind (about 40 in all) are in East Anglia in the region of Cambridge, Peterborough and Norwich, and made of Barnack stone. The most numerous find of these cross-slabs was made in 1811 beneath the earthworks of Cambridge Castle, which was built by the Normans around the year 1070 on the graveyard of an Anglo-Saxon monastery. A similar slab, illustrated here, exists at Peterborough Cathedral, and comparable stones without interlace patterns are known from Sussex at Chithurst, Steyning and Stedham.

Many ancient churches and abbeys contain ancient crosses and cross-slabs. Their state of preservation and the conditions under which they are kept varies greatly. More often than not, they seem merely to be an inconvenience for the church authorities, so they are relegated to dusty corners inside the building, or languish outside in stone-heaps behind chicken wire amid gardening tools and refuse. The historical significance of the stones seems not to affect the way they are handled: even the monuments of kings are treated in this manner. Perhaps the least threatened are those stones actually built into the fabric, like the pieces of Celtic Cross in the walls of many churches, such as Little St Mary's in Cambridge and Llangeinwen in Anglesey. Such stones as these are visible, but it is clear that there are many more ancient carved stones embedded invisibly in the fabric of churches, castles, bridges and sea walls. Numerous fine examples came to light at Bakewell in Derbyshire in 1841, when the tower and transepts of the church were demolished during reconstruction. Sculptured stones removed from the old building included around 300 ancient monuments, ranging in date from before the Norman conquest to the thirteenth century. Seventy of them were retained, and built into the south porch of the church, but the rest were re-used and buried in the new walls, without being recorded in any way. Thus, a remarkable opportunity was lost, for many of those still visible show the many variant forms that the wheel-cross took. With the present decline of religion, however, many ancient churches are likely to be demolished in the near future, and doubtless more fascinating ancient stones will emerge again, if we who are interested in our heritage remain alert to developments.

Pictish Stones and Crosses

Before the immigration of the Scots from Ireland, the Picts of northern Britain possessed their own style of Celtic art. Although the Picts probably produced wonderful textiles, leatherwork, woodwork and metalwork, little has survived, and it is almost entirely through memorial stones that their art is known. J. Romilly Allen, who made an intensive study of Pictish memorial stones (*The Early Christian Monuments of Scotland*, The Pinkfoot Press, 1993) classified them into three categories. His Class I stones, which may date from the seventh century, are natural, largely unworked, megaliths upon which various emblems or 'symbols' were carved. As the meaning or symbolism of these emblems is unknown, it is rather paradoxical that the name usually given to the stones on which they appear is 'symbol stones'. However, by drawing parallels with the customs of tattooing warriors in other cultures, it may be surmised that the tattoos worn by the Picts were in the form of such 'symbols', made in honour of the gods. As in many warrior societies, it is likely that each Pictish warrior was known by his unique personal array of tattoos, which were reproduced on his memorial stone when he died.

Around the middle of the eighth century, Pictish stonecarvers began to use the cross in their designs, and Biblical images began to enter their repertoire of images. Romilly Allen's definition of these Class II Pictish stones categorizes them as: 'erect cross-slabs or recumbent coped stones with symbols [sic] and Celtic ornament sculptured in relief.' Although the cross is a significant part of the design of these stones, there are no known representations of the crucifixion or indeed of any images that can be interpreted as representing episodes from the New Testament. These are the monuments that were set up after the acceptance of Northumbrian Catholicism in the year 710 by the Pictish high king Nechtan IV mac Derile.

The Class II slabs have crosses whose form and content is related to contemporary known manuscripts and probably also tapestries, now lost. Fourteen variants of cross have been identified, the most common of which have rounded indentations at the crossing in the manner of the four-holed crosses. Equally prevalent is the rectilinear cross composed of squares, with squares at the crossing. Similar varieties were made in Ireland. There are fine examples on stones at Clonmacnois, Durrow and elsewhere. Among the earliest in this style are the Pictish stones from Aberlemno churchyard, Birsay, Meigle, Papil, Rossie Priory and St Vigeans. All have sculpture in relatively low relief, including Pictish emblems of the Pagan period, perhaps reproducing the tattoos of the dead. Development of the style led, around the year 800, to more complex work. The Hilton of Cadboll stone in Easter Ross is a good example. It is carved with scenes from Biblical mythology, hunting figures and Pictish emblems. The whole emblematical scheme of these stones is syncretic, with elements from many sources. Certain elements come from indigenous Pictish Paganism. The Biblical figures may have been influenced by Mercian art, while the monsters and demons have similarities with those described in the early illustrated text, *The Marvels of the East*, which was current in Northumbrian monasteries at the time.

At Rossie Priory, in Tayside, is a stone sometimes called a 'page in stone'. Frequently, the design of this stone is assumed to be a sculptural representation of a page of a book. Equally, however, it could represent one of the woven textile banners that were used by travelling priests in conjunction with portable altars. There are parallels, too, with the Pagan memorial stones of Gotland. The whole stone has an interlace border which merges with the three free arms of the cross at the left, right and top. The centre of the cross is a circle with key-patterns in the middle, while the cross-shaft bears carvings of horseriders. In the panels surrounding the cross are depictions of various things: an angel, or fury; a human figure holding the necks of two birds in the manner of ancient images of the goddess Artemis, Lady of the Beasts; a hound, horsemen and other animals. There are only a few Pictish stones of this type that show the typical Pictish images on the front of the cross-slab. At this period, it was more usual to carve them on the rear of the slab. Possibly, converted Picts who still wore the old Pagan tattoos, or still honoured them as ancestral heraldry, were commemorated thus. The typically 'Pictish' images on this slab are a crescent-and-rod and the enigmatic stylized beast variously described as a hippogriff, elephant, seahorse or walrus.

In the churchyard at Aberlemno in Tayside is one of the most famous Pictish cross-slabs, which amalgamates the slab-form with the wheel-headed Celtic Cross. The slab is sculptured so that the cross-form stands out strongly from the background. The upright panel that would be the shaft if the cross were free-standing is carved with a complex interlace pattern based on three circles. This 'supports' the lower part of the wheel-cross, which is carved as though it were separate, being distinguished by a more open, separate interlace pattern. The cross-arms on either side of the centre bear key-patterns, while the centre is composed of six spirals around a seventh, central, one. The cross is topped with an X-formed interlace. One of the four 'holes' in the cross has been drilled right through, making it a holed stone. This hole destroys part of the carving on the back, showing it to be a later, vernacular, addition for magical purposes. The supporting slab is carved with spiralling animal-ornament, and the cross's top is flanked by two stylized beasts. Other notable Pictish cross-slabs of this style include those from Glamis, carved with fine interlace and beasts, at Scoonie and at Meigle.

Later in the ninth century, the so-called 'boss style' was developed. This is characterized by an adventurous departure in design employing large round bosses sculpted with interlace, which are sometimes accompanied by serpents. These serpentine bosses may be a representation of the magical druidic 'serpents' eggs' or 'adder stones' mentioned by Pliny in his *Natural History*: 'In the summer, numerous snakes entwine themselves in a ball, held together by a secretion from their bodies and by spittle ... the druids value it highly. It is said to ensure success in lawsuits and a favourable reception with princes.' Whatever the meaning of bosses, the style was used on slabs in the Isle of Man and free-standing crosses in western Scotland, Iona and Ireland. Among the notable examples of Pictish stones in the 'boss style' are the Roadside Cross at Aberlemno, the cross from Nigg in Easter Ross in Highland Region, another at Shandwick nearby, and the Pictish shrine at St Andrews. The Nigg stone has remarkably fine carvings, and bosses composed variously of knotwork of serpentine and rectilinear form, and spirals. This highly elaborate, sophisticated and doubtless very expensive style was not maintained for long. Soon, stonemasons adopted more simplified designs, examples of which can be seen in the stones from Fowlis Wester, Tayside and Rosemarkie in the Highland Region.

A Pictish stone from Dunfallandy in Tayside has a cross based upon squares, but with rounded forms at the angles of the cross. These rounded forms appear at the top of the shaft beneath the cross-head, which is in more prominent relief than the rest of the carvings. Each of the four arms of the cross-head is sculpted with prominent bosses, five each on the upright parts and three each on the cross-arms. Panels of spiralwork form the background to the bosses, while the whole slab is bordered by interlacework in the manner of the Gotland stones. Between the border and the cross are ten panels bearing beasts and angels. The back of the slab is purely pictorial, with horsemen, dogs, a centaur with twin axes, beasts and a man who stands between four animals, often interpreted as representing Daniel among the lions.

The stones later classified as Pictish Class III came into being in the late ninth century after the unification of Pictland and Dalriada by King Kenneth mac Alpin. These Class III stones are in the form of free-standing crosses and cross-slabs. They differ from the earlier slabs because the Pictish emblems are absent. Perhaps, because by now they considered themselves to be wholly Christian, those commemorated by the stones no longer bore their identifying tattoos or honoured the old heraldry of their ancestors. Also, because they are slabs, these stones differ from the contemporary free-standing wheel-headed crosses of the Celtic church. It is likely that when King Nechtan IV mac Derile adopted Catholic Christianity from the Anglians of Northumbria and expelled the Celtic priesthood from Pictland, it was considered to be politically expedient not to use the Celtic Cross, which had clear Irish origins. Instead, the Pictish masons developed a national style that served as an emblem of their religious allegiance to Rome rather than Ireland. As a national style, it was maintained long after Dalriada and Pictland became Scotland.

At Dupplin, west of Perth, Anglian influence is apparent in the sculptures of vinescrolls and beasts. There is similar ornament on the cross at Crieff in Tayside. Mustachioed men resembling those on Muiredach's Cross at Monasterboice are on the Dupplin cross, and on a cross-slab at Benvie, Tayside. They may represent Scots rather than Picts, who were shown bearded. A cross-slab from Inchbrayock, Tayside, has a squared cross on one side, accompanied by figures, interlace and a beast. The rear, as with so many Pictish stones, has human figures engaged in hunting and Biblical scenes. The interlace and spirals on the Inchbrayock stone, like much Pictish carving of this period, is a free and dynamic interpretation of the underlying geometrical matrix.

There are few known Pictish stones that are carved with the crucified Christ. A cross-shaft from Monifieth near Dundee has a crucifixion, but on a stone influenced by Anglo-Danish tradition. It is possible that before the unification of the Picts and Scots there were no such representations. It is equally possible, however, that early Pictish depictions of the crucifixion have all been destroyed, for many stones were damaged or smashed in the suppression of Catholic worship in the sixteenth century. An idea of what happened can be seen on a Pictish cross-slab from Woodwray on Tayside which has had the cross carefully chipped away, leaving only its surrounding beasts and border. So it is not unlikely that Protestant zealots, in attempting to extirpate what they considered to be idolatry, destroyed all of the Pictish stones that bore images of the crucifixion, giving us a false impression of the actual practices of the Pictish masons.

Chapter 7

FORM AND PATTERN IN CELTIC ART

Structurally, Celtic art is based upon a hidden, but ever-present geometric basis. Sacred geometry has been practised in the British Isles since the time of the megalith builders. When building in dressed stone was introduced from Roman-influenced lands, a complementary sacred geometry, originating ultimately in ancient Egypt, was added to the indigenous tradition. Knowledge of sacred geometry was part of the trade secrets of the mason, and couched in esoteric terms impenetrable to the layperson. Plutarch stated that the Egyptian priests and priestesses carried three sacred rods, dedicated respectively to Isis, Osiris and Horus. The rod of Isis represented origination, and was coloured black. The rod of Osiris signified the receptive principle, being coloured red. Horus's rod was blue, symbolizing the result of combination. They were ascribed the numbers 5, 4 and 3. When they were brought together, a right-angled triangle was formed.

This is the basis of the 47th proposition of Euclid, the geometrical theorem associated with Pythagoras, which proves how any triangle the sides of which measure 3, 4 and 5 units contains a right angle. Although it may seem deceptively simple, it was not common knowledge in earlier times, being a closely guarded secret of initiates of the mystery schools. Nevertheless it is the fundamental basis of all geometry. In medieval Britain, this mystery was embodied in the device known as the Druids' Cord or *snor*, a rope with 12 knots dividing it into 13 equal sections which was used in land measure and building to lay out right angles on the ground. The *snor* and mystic rod can be seen in old illustrations of master masons from the middle ages, and Sir Christopher Wren's ceremonial measuring rod is preserved in St Paul's Cathedral in London. He used it in the foundation and completion ceremonies of the great sacred building.

Geometry and Symbolism

Laying out anything by geometry is a symbolic re-creation of the world. Because of this, ancient traditions portray the creator as the supreme geometer of the universe. Signifying the works of the great architect of the universe, in the shape of law and order, authority and justice, the rectilinear grid is present in Celtic art. It served to depict holy figures in both the Pagan and Christian traditions. The back of an image of the horned god Cernunnos from Roqueperteuse in southern France has a grid in the form of four squares within another square. Repeating cross-patterns based on the grid were being carved on Celtic stones 600 years before the Christian religion came into being. Tesselations of T-shapes with crosses can be seen in Germany on Celtic memorials dating from the La Tène period. The lower piece of a stone image in human form, found at Steinenbronn in Baden-Württemberg and now kept in the Württembergisches Landesmuseum in Stuttgart, is carved with designs that were used again on Christian artefacts in the British Isles. A thousand years later, an evangelist in the *Book of Durrow* wears a cloak with a grid pattern upon it.

Played on a gridded board, the Celtic game known as *Tawlbwrdd* in Wales, and *Fidcheall* or *Brannumh* in Ireland, was more than just a pastime, for it symbolized the land and the royal order necessary for its proper functioning according to divine laws. Because of this, one of the official emblems of the judge in ancient Wales was a *Tawlbwrdd* board. As the ruling principle, the rectilinear grid underlies Celtic artwork on stone crosses and manuscripts. Just as good laws and just administration of a land should be apparent only through the proper functioning of society, so the guiding grid of Celtic art is usually just an underlying principle invisible in the finished artwork.

The men who made the Celtic high crosses were the best stonemasons of their day. Their craft is evident both in the actual construction of the high crosses from several pieces of stone, fitted together in a masterly manner; and in the use of geometry in their design. Their Celtic understanding of geometry was masterful, evident in the interlace and spiral designs not only of stone crosses but also of illuminated manuscripts, metalwork and stonecarving. Here, the Christian tradition did not extirpate the earlier Pagan vision, but continued and developed it. The geometric grid that underlies a considerable amount of surviving ornament on Celtic Crosses is of one or other of two basic forms, the square or diamond. The construction of both patterns was one of the fundamental mysteries of ancient geometry.

According to ancient British Bardic teachings, beneath the outer, visible form of matter lies a subtle matrix upon which all things are based. The old Welsh word *manred* denotes this invisible matrix of existence; the atoms and molecules, the structures and geometrical relationships that make up physical reality. These patterns are not eternally fixed, but flow through time, expressing its essence through an almost infinite variety of forms. More than any other art form, Celtic art displays these ever-changing dynamic patterns of *manred*. Like nature, the geometric matrices upon which Celtic tesselations, spirals and knotwork are based are continuous. In their plurality, all of the different pattern-styles are infinitely interchangeable. They can easily fade into one another imperceptibly. The patterns of *manred* are infinitely changing, but they are not meaningless. Thus, esoterically, the patterns of Celtic art are the fixed artistic representations of the ever-flowing particles of *manred*, for all is flux.

Celtic artists use the principle of self-similarity in conjunction with the underlying geometry of Celtic art. This is where a form at one size is included within a similar form on a larger scale. This principle, recognized in Europe over 3,000 years ago by the people of the Hallstatt culture, was re-affirmed by Benoit Mandelbrot in 1980 when he discovered fractal mathematics. Self-similarity is the innate quality of an integral structure that manifests itself as repeating patterns from the smallest level to the largest. Thus, the smallest part of existence, the microcosm, is linked to the largest, the macrocosm. This link is not a crude reflection, but a more subtle, ordered repetition through the middle ground that lies between the small and the large. Self-similarity means that a structure that is present at one level is repeated on both higher and lower levels. Thus, the overall pattern of a Celtic artefact may be repeated again in the details of the ornament upon it. Just as there is no place for a void middle ground in nature, so in Celtic art there are no empty spaces, just as there are no blank spaces in the cosmos. Structure is present at every point, with each small part simultaneously reflecting the essential structure of the whole. Thus, all is inseparable. This essential oneness has been the guiding principle of Celtic art from its emergence 2,700 years ago until the present day. It is the *leitmotif* of the Celtic Cross.

Self-similarity is apparent throughout Celtic art. The magnificent bull-headed torc found at Trichtingen in Germany is a fine example of how the principle of self-similarity operates. Each of the bull-head terminals on the torc wears a torc around its neck, the terminals of which are torcs, and so on. In Christian Ireland, the same principle was observed in the construction of shrines which were contained in identical, but larger, sacred containers, which themselves were kept in churches of the same form. In turn, the churches were designed symbolically to be images of the body of Christ and also the form of God's creation, the cosmos.

Techniques and Ornamentation

Many researchers into Celtic Crosses have emphasized the close relationship between the designs used on ornamental metalwork and stone sculpture. It is evident that small items of metalwork, whether sacred objects, ornaments, jewellery or weapons, were easily transported from place to place and thus could serve as models for craftspeople in localities distant from their places of origin. Thus, new artistic styles could be disseminated as small objects. However, we should remember that while much metalwork has survived from the first millennium the undoubtedly more common wooden, bone, ivory, textile and leather items were not as durable and have decayed. Only a few have been preserved until the present day. So when we look at metalwork, we are seeing only one part of the repertoire of Celtic craftspeople.

Christian elements of design may have been disseminated into Celtic art before the religious beliefs to which they refer. When Christian elements such as the *chi-rho*, cross and fish appear in metalwork or other art of this conversion period, it is not a certain sign that the makers or owners were members of the religion. Today in everyday life we can see people wearing crosses and crucifixes as lucky charms, along with ankhs, yang-and-yin signs, Stars of David, pentagrams and Hammers of Thor, among other sacred amulets. Perhaps, however, the majority of those who wear these do so for reasons of adornment in a pluralistic culture rather than as part of any personal belief. Similarly, in the past, when a craftsperson took a Christian motif from a textile or a pot, he or she may have done so because the design had magically protective connotations, rather than for ideological reasons. The same applies, of course, to exotic Pagan motifs.

There is much evidence of religious and artistic syncretism in the post-Roman period. For instance, at the Mark of Mote, a fortified town on the edge of Dalbeattie Forest in Kirkcudbrightshire, archaeologists have excavated cosmopolitan metalworking workshops dating from the sixth and seventh centuries. There, Celtic and Anglian crafts-people co-operated at a centre of excellence, making brooches and other small items in bronze, brass and gold. The artefacts made there incorporated contemporary elements from indigenous Celtic art, as well as Germanic motifs and interlace patterns from the eastern Mediterranean. Glass was brought in from Germanic workshops else-where, for use in enamel-making. Items of Mark of Mote style were exported across the sea to Ulster. Cosmopolitan centres such as this were places where differing traditions could be integrated to produce new ideas and styles. It is to them that we must look for the formative elements which went to make up the phenomenon of the Celtic Cross.

Certain cross-slabs, made in the period before free-standing stone crosses, depict the actual cross as an element of a picture, as if the cross is standing in the landscape. Often, they stand above scenes of hunting or battle, and the otherworldly 'haunted tanglewood', in which men fight serpents and dragons. Because these representations pre-date the erection of stone crosses, then the crosses they depict must have been made of some other material, either of wood, or, in the case of small ones at least, from plaitwork made of grass, straw, rushes, osiers or hazel wands. It is indisputable that interlace patterns have their origin in the plaiting of materials, such as in ropework and basketry, hurdle-making and the braiding of hair.

Until the invention of wire fencing, wattle hurdles of woven hazel were made all over the Celtic realms. Primarily known as components of fences and screens, as early as the neolithic period, trackways of hurdles were made across swampy ground, such as the Somerset Levels. The present Irish name of Dublin, Baile átha Cliath, means 'the town of the hurdle-ford'. Wattle hurdles also served as walling elements in timberframe buildings and as fish weirs. Panels of Celtic interlace work on stone carvings resemble closely the patterns employed in wattle-weaving. Ribbonwork with a central line may depict the split hazel branches from which hurdles are woven, for the actual objects have this appearance. Each region of the British Isles has its own traditional wattle-forms, expressed through the variant weaving-patterns of the 'middle binding'. Perhaps some Celtic interlaces on crosses are messages in ogham.

The better-known corn dollies and other small plaited work are made throughout the Celtic lands at certain times of year, and it is unlikely that this is not the continuation of a very ancient ancestral practice. They vary in complexity, with the simplest designs being made from only two strands, but for more complicated work four, five or even six strands are needed. In Ireland, Harvest Knots are made from the straw taken at the harvest, to be worn as buttonholes for the harvest fair. Other harvest straw emblems include the stellar 'harvest stars' and the numerous forms of corn dollies. Straw-plaiting is an ancient craft, the techniques and patterns of which have been handed down through the generations. The straws are plaited from the base in a spiral, one over the next, gradually building up a three-dimensional body of the required shape. This is the method for making the St Bridget's Cross, which, along with the simpler but related Palm Sunday crosses, is an example of plaitwork which still retains its sacred connotations.

In keeping with making a holy artefact, there are a number of prescriptions that must be observed in making St Bridget's Crosses. They must be made on St Bridget's Eve, after sunset on the last day of January. St Bridget's Day marks the commencement of the pastoral year. Rushes must be pulled up, not cut, and the weaving must be done sunwise, from left to right. There are a number of patterns for St Bridget's Crosses, but the most common is in the form of four equal arms, set on the edge. Putting a St Bridget's Cross above the door brings holy protection from the risk of fire and other misfortunes that might befall the household. There is also a three-armed form of the cross, the triskele, which is used today only to protect cowsheds, though it is the basis of the emblem of the Isle of Man. The plaited straw charm called *Bratóg Brighde* (Bridget's Rag) is a protection against storms at sea, carried by the Donegal fishermen of Tory Island. Another common form that St Bridget's Cross can take is an interlace of six elements that makes a binding knot. This shows affinities with the Swabian and Tyrolean magical protector known as a *Schratterlgatterl*, which is an interweaving of a number of sticks employed as a barrier beyond which evil spirits cannot pass. Interlaces like this appear frequently in the patterns on Celtic crosses, while some Welsh and Manx crosses have designs that reproduce in stone the plaited patterns of whole crosses that are made from grass, rushes or straw, some of which are the classical Celtic Cross within the wheel. In County Galway, such 'woven crosses' are put in the rafters of the house at Hallowe'en to protect it and the family against demonic intrusion. Another form of St Bridget's Cross is in the shape of a square plaited on a cross of sticks. These straw-square patterns are made at Christmastime in Sweden and in Estonia, where they are worn on hats, and on the straw masks used in guising games.

Although they are carved from stone, many crosses have

the appearance of structures made from less durable material, perhaps wickerwork or wood. Some stone crosses seem to be representations of wooden crosses upon which panels have been fixed. Therefore it is frequently suggested that many early permanent free-standing crosses were made of wood, perhaps with separate panels on the outside. Perhaps the interlace patterns on stone crosses reproduce the actual plaitwork of wickerwork that was attached both as adornment and magical protection against evil spirits. It is probable that, in Pagan days, woven sacred objects or poetic wattles resembling St Bridget's Crosses were hung on holy trees. Later, when crosses were set up, the sacred weavings were fixed to the cross instead.

In addition to panelwork made of plaited material, it is often suggested that metal panels were also used, where the patron was wealthy enough to commission them. However attractive this theory may seem, no large metal panels of this type are known, and the relative scarcity of metal in pre-industrial times makes it very unlikely that there were large wooden crosses sheathed in bronze. Attaching separate panels to larger artefacts was a common technique in Europe at that period, where craftspeople fixed cast or hammered panels bearing protective images of divine beings to helmets, armour and sacred objects. Many examples of this principle survive in the Celtic area, but they are all fairly small.

Elements of woodworking technique can be seen in representations of crosses, such as the cross visible on a buttress of the church at Llangeinwen in Anglesey, or that at St Laurence's Church at Papil in Shetland. Staff-crosses ending in a spoke are depicted on slabs at Clonmacnois in County Offaly, Trowbridge in Wiltshire, and Hansted, near Aarhus in Denmark. A Celtic cross-slab re-used at a later date for part of the church fabric, the Llangeinwen cross is shown with a pointed foot, resembling a spike. It has been suggested that this shows a wooden cross, with its means of insertion in the ground, but we can never know how large this cross was meant to be. Perhaps it represents a small processional cross the size of a priest's crozier, rather than one of high-cross dimensions. There are actual contemporary illustrations of hand-held crosses for processional and ceremonial use. The north cross at Ahenny has a sculpted panel showing a funeral procession led by a priest carrying a portable wheel-headed cross. The eighth-century *Lichfield Gospels*, otherwise known as the *Gospels of St Chad*, have an illuminated page showing an evangelist holding crossed staves in the 'Osiris' position. Unfortunately, the ravages of time have destroyed all of the crosses of this type, made of wood and metal, which once existed in every church.

Many of the later, larger crosses, assembled from several separate pieces of stone, were put together with mortise-and-tenon joints, usually associated with wood-joinery rather than that of European stonemasonry. It can be argued, however, that because such joints in stone were used in megalithic times at Stonehenge and elsewhere, they may represent the deliberate use of an archaic technique as sacral craftsmanship. This deliberate sacred archaism appears in certain essential elements of Classical architecture. Some stone crosses, such as St Martin's Cross on Iona, also have enigmatic slots that may have accommodated wooden extensions that held ribbons, banners or woven emblems. Crosses with a circular shaft, such as the Wolverhampton Pillar and the Gosforth Cross, have patterns that resemble the tree bark left at the basal portion of some contemporary maypoles in Germany. This may recall the creation of crosses from whole trees, but equally may be derived from the patterns carved on the lower portions of Roman Jupiter Columns. Until an intact ancient wooden standing cross is found, these opposing interpretations will have equal plausibility.

Chapter 8

CROSS STYLES

There are many examples of different styles of Celtic Cross throughout the British Isles, from Cornwall and the Isles of Scilly to Wales, the Isle of Man, northern England and Scotland. These are described in detail below.

Welsh Crosses

There are around 450 ancient sculptured stones, crosses and allied monuments known in Wales. Stylistic analysis of surviving early stones indicates that there were individual guilds of sculptors at various important monasteries, each of which worked in their own particular recognizable styles. Thus, antiquaries have been able to identify a number of distinct schools of ancient Welsh cross sculpture. In Glamorgan, for example, there were three major workshops: at Llantwit Major, Margam and Merthyr Mawr. Their examples account for around half of the known Welsh crosses. Other recognizable sculptural workshops existed at St David's in Dyfed and at Penmon Priory on Anglesey in Gwynedd, areas that, unlike Glamorgan, were within the sphere of Irish influence. Before the ninth century, the Welsh did not use the more complex standing crosses favoured in Ireland, Scotland and the north of England. Then, under royal and ecclesiastical patronage, cross-slabs and high crosses comparable with them began to appear. Ring-headed crosses exist only in the north of Wales. Round-shafted pillar-crosses are found in north and central Wales, while wheel-crosses and allied forms are restricted to the south of the country.

The school of Glamorgan produced a characteristic form of Celtic Cross, known as the 'panelled' or 'cartwheel' slab, which were made from the late ninth century until the eleventh century. The finest example, preserved in the Margam Stones Museum, is a rectangular slab 193 cm (76 in) tall. The top half is carved with an eight-spoked wheel, in which the spokes are arranged irregularly in pairs to make a splayed cross-pattern. There is a boss at the centre of the wheel that makes the whole composition resemble a shield. Surrounding the wheel-cross is ornamental carving containing spirals. The lower panel of the stone is inscribed with a text in Latin commemorating a certain Ilquici. A later form of cross, which developed also on the Isle of Man, is the 'disc-headed' cross. The Margam Stones Museum keeps a fine example, though this is broken and not all of it remains. Known as the Conbelin Cross, it was found at Margam Abbey and dates from around the turn of the tenth century. Set on a rectangular stone block, which has the usual horsemen at the hunt, and just a hint of the stepped 'holy mountain' form, the shaft and disc-head were carved from a single block of Pennant Sandstone. The disc-head is sculpted with a five-square cross which overlaps the interlace-bearing ring. At the centre of the middle square is a circular boss that gives the disc the resemblance to a round shield, as with the Ilquici slab. Like some other south Welsh crosses of this period, the Conbelin cross was carved with a Latin inscription. Although damaged, it probably reads 'Conbelin set up this cross for the soul of Ric'. Inscriptions on these old Welsh crosses are often set low down, and it is possible that this is so that devotees could see them while kneeling in prayer at the foot of the crosses.

Kept in the church at Llantwit Major, under less than ideal conditions amid a jumble of chairs, tables, other carved stones and coffin lids, are no fewer than three ancestral memorials dedicated to the souls of south Welsh royalty. They are the monuments of-King Samson, King Juthahel and Res, father of King Houelt. Llantwit Major, called in Welsh Llanilltyd Fawr after its founder, St Illtyd, was the sacred burial-ground of the local kings. It is a great pity that these royal memorials are not honoured properly in their own land. The Samson cross bears the words (in Latin): 'Samson set up this cross for his soul, Iltut, of Samson the King, of Samuel and Ebisar'; while the cross of King Juthahel states: 'In the name of God most high begins the Cross of the Saviour, which Abbot Samson prepared for his own soul and for the soul of King Juthahel and Artmail and Tecain.' The Houelt Cross is a cross made of local gritstone for the ruler of the local kingdom of Glywysing, Hywel ap Rhys, who was a vassal of King Alfred the Great of Wessex in the year 884. It bears the Latin inscription: 'In the name of God the Father, and of the Son, and of the Holy Spirit, this cross Houelt prepared for the soul of his father, Res.' Its supporting 'shaft' is inscribed with a tesselation of triangular key-patterns, and the wheel-head is composed of an equal-armed cross made from five squares, set within and overlapping a ring of single-band interlace. The four spaces between the arms of the cross are solid, and filled with three-fold interlace. Beneath a wooden awning in the churchyard at Llangan in South Glamorgan is another notable south Welsh cross-slab. Dating from around the same period as the Houelt Cross, it bears a representation of the crucifixion, of which only a few are known from this period in Wales.

Among the stones in the church at Llantwit Major is an unusual pillar, carved from sandstone. In former times, it was set in the ground outside the north wall of the church. As a pillar, it is unusual because it has a straight, vertical groove running down the back, the function of which is unknown. The zigzag and interlace patterns on the pillar are thus not continuous, but in distinct, if curved, panels. Unlike the common Celtic Cross, whose shaft is square or rectangular in cross-section, round pillars are extremely rare. There is only one other Celtic round pillar in Wales, that of Eliseg's Pillar, near Valle Crucis Abbey in north Wales. In England, the Wolverhampton Pillar is perhaps the closest parallel. These rare pillars are the spiritual successors of the Roman columns sacred to Jupiter. Another remarkable Celtic pillar exists *in situ* in the churchyard of Llandough, near Cardiff, which is perhaps the site of the ancient monastic enclosure mentioned in 'The Life of St Cadog' (*The Lives of the British Saints*). The pillar is of a type unknown elsewhere, for it consists of four separate pieces of stone, set one upon the other. An inscription dedicates this monument to a person named Irbic. It is dated from around the millennium. The pillar's base is rather conventional. It resembles those of Irish crosses, being a rectangular pyramid with a carving of interlace, a horse and rider and a man's bust. From this rises a tapering column that has rounded pilasters carved with interlace at the four corners, with interlaced panels between them. This is topped by a small capital which supports a cushion-shaped stone whose carving makes it resemble a stack of ropes. The upper part of this cushion-stone is shaped like a cross base, and from it rises another shaft, four-sided and ornamented with interlace. The top is broken, though a similar upper portion exists nearby at Llandaff in South Glamorgan.

The former county of Pembrokeshire has several notable crosses, of which three are exceptional by any standards. The church at Penally, near Tenby, contains two crosses, one broken and one intact. The broken cross-shaft is a fragment that interlaces beasts in an even more Anglian style. The intact cross at Penally is far more impressive, for it shows the Celtic expertise in multivalent art, especially in the masterly way that the interlace pattern on the lower part of the cross becomes a vinescroll on the upper. Here, the underlying geometry of the interlace is re-interpreted by the sculptor as the structure upon which the vine is based. The vinescroll here, derived ultimately from the Roman Jupiter Columns, with its interlaced tendrils and double-beaded stem, resembles closely those on crosses in the Northumbrian region of influence. The cross's wheel-head is perforated by four holes that go right through the stone, and it is outlined by cable-mouldings.

The original base of the cross can still be seen *in situ* in the churchyard to the west of the church. In 1956, the Ancient Monuments Board For Wales recommended that, where possible, ancient sculptured stones and crosses should be taken indoors. Then, many stones were removed from their proper locations, marking the burial-places of the dead, to become instead indoor 'art objects'. Neither has the result of this action been a complete success. In 1995, I was told by a church warden at Penally that, since it had been removed into the church, the intact cross has deteriorated, owing possibly to the effects of heating and the smoke from candles. Although in some cases it may protect them from further erosion by polluted air, removal of crosses from their original locations not only denies the very intention of their makers, and seriously diminishes the historical reality of the place, but may also threaten the continued existence of the cross itself.

In a roadside niche in the wall surrounding the ruined Carew Castle is the 4.12-metres (13 ½-ft) high cross dedicated, according to its inscription, to King Margiteut, son of Etguin. Known by his modern Welsh name, Meredudd ap Edwin was king of Deheubarth (this part of Wales) from 1033 to 1035. The cross is composed of two stones, the lower of which combines base and shaft. T-shaped key-patterns, diagonal knotwork, the inscription panel, irregular key-patterns and more regular looped knotwork, containing two circles. The head is made as a separate piece, like its counterpart at Nevern. Dating from around the turn of the first millennium, the Nevern churchyard cross stands 3.96 metres (13 ft) high. The head of the Nevern cross, like that at Carew, was carved from a separate stone, being fixed to the shaft by means of mortise-and-tenon joints in the manner of Stonehenge. There are two short inscriptions, one of which reads 'DNS', being an abbreviation of the Latin word *Dominus* (Master or Lord). All four sides of the cross are illustrated here. In the church, a stained-glass window representing the founder, St Brynach, has an anachronistic representation of the Nevern Cross behind him, above which flies a dove.

Also dating from around the first millennium, and located west of Whitford in Clwyd, stands Maen Achwyfan, 'The Stone of Lamentations'. This is a monolithic cross 3.4 metres (11 ft) in height. Ornamented with spirals, the X-shaped 'Pagan Cross' and irregular net-like interlace, the design of Maen Achwyfan shows affinities with Northumbrian work. The circular wheel-head is surrounded by two rings of ropelike beading, and has a cross with interlaced arms that merge with a third, inner, ring. At the very centre is a tightly interlaced central boss with a cross at the middle. One of the carvings is of an ithyphallic man.

Close to the eisteddfod town of Llangollen and the ruined Cistercian abbey of Valle Crucis (Valley of the Cross) is the Pillar of Eliseg. It has no head; only a round, treelike shaft remains. Formerly the cross had an inscription, recorded in 1696, that commemorated the erection of the cross by King Cyngen, in honour and praise of Eliseg, his great-grandfather. Cyngen, who died in the year 854, was the last king of an independent state of Powys. Today, the Pillar of Eliseg bears an inscription commemorating T. Lloyd, who, in 1779, re-erected the fallen and broken cross-shaft. On Anglesey, Penmon Priory, which may occupy the former location of the holiest shrine of the druids, contains two interesting disc-headed crosses. Dating from around the millennium, they show Norse influence, being close in their design to the crosses in the church of St John in Chester, the product of a Norse sculptural school. The motif of the temptation of St Anthony, or at least a man in combat with demons, appears on one of the crosses.

Powys has several notable cross-slabs. One of the most interesting is at Llandyfaelog Fach. Dating from the tenth century, it bears the name Briamail Flou, and has one of the few known representations of an ancient Welsh nobleman or warrior. Bearded and standing proud, Briamail holds a club across his right shoulder, while his left hand is on the hilt of a sword. Apart from being a useful weapon in the northern European martial arts, the wooden club called a *baculum* was a symbol of office. As commander-in-chief of the Norman army, William of Normandy carried one at the Battle of Hastings, as later field-marshals carry their baton. Above Briamail is a simple cross formed of an interlaced single band. Surrounding the lord and the cross are various types of knotwork and key-patterns, while the inscription is bordered by ropelike banding. Another cross-slab, kept in the church at Meifod in Powys, has a remarkable carving of a form of Christian ankh, which resembles Coptic models. Possibly the lid of a sarcophagus, in which case it resembles Merovingian parallels in France, it is sculpted with two crosses. One is a conventional cross carved with interlace motifs. At the centre of the cross is a four-fold knot with a circular middle. Above this cross, and connected to it by a rod is a wheel-cross upon which Christ is crucified. In the four quarters between the spokes of the wheel are bosses. The rest of the composition is filled with knots and beasts without any overall pattern.

The most holy Celtic Cross of Wales was the Cross Gneth, a precious reliquary that enshrined a small part of the True Cross. Formerly in the possession of the princes of north

Wales, it was taken to England by King Edward I in 1283. When he founded the Order of the Garter in 1348, King Edward III gave the Cross Gneth to the chapel of the Order at Windsor Castle, where it was enshrined as its most precious relic. Although the cross itself disappeared from St George's Chapel in 1548, when its gold back was sold, we know what it looked like. There is a carving of the Cross Gneth on a stone roof boss at the eastern end of the south choir aisle of the chapel. It portrays King Edward I and Bishop Beauchamp kneeling in adoration of the relic, which is a classic Celtic Cross. To all who knelt at the cross, which was taller than a man, 40 days' pardon for sins was granted.

Cornwall and the Scilly Isles

It has been estimated that Cornwall has some 500 standing crosses or fragments, dating from between the ninth and the fifteenth centuries. This is a very high number for a relatively small area. More crosses seem to have survived in this county than elsewhere in England, perhaps because of its Celtic traditions where sacred places belonged to families rather than the church. In parts of England and Wales where the Celtic tradition had been weakened or extirpated, crosses belonged to the church, and when Roman Catholicism was suppressed at the Reformation they were destroyed. In predominantly Celtic areas like Cornwall, however, individual crosses actually belonged to individual families, and could not so easily be pulled down.

Cornish crosses tend to be rather simpler than those in other parts of the British Isles, owing perhaps to the hardness of the local stone – granite – that was used to make them. They have three distinct types. Some are round-headed pillar-stones; others are Latin crosses carved from a single stone; others are wheel-headed crosses, often drilled through with four holes between the arms. Of the round-headed variety, there are ten main types of carved cross – six use crosses within circles, and the others have various unencircled kinds of cross carved onto them. Some round-headed cross-pillars are carved with the crucified Christ, but without a cross. The positions of the body vary greatly, and comparable figures exist on wheel-headed crosses. Many of the later crosses have Celtic interlace patterns comparable with known examples in other parts of the British Isles, as well as geometric ornament that resembles Anglo-Norman grave-slab work in England and Wales. The variety of Cornish crosses is a remarkable tribute to the inventiveness of their artists.

Most surviving Cornish crosses date from between the eleventh and thirteenth centuries. In the thirteenth century, there was a resurgence of crossmaking in the older style, such as the cross at Quethioc, where medieval 'gothic' influence is modified by simplified vinescroll patterns. Because Cornwall was not conquered by the Anglo-Saxons until the year 925, it retained the older Romanized Celtic culture, maintaining links by sea with Wales to the north, the Isles of Scilly to the west and Brittany to the south. Cornwall thus has a number of wheel-head crosses the designs of which are related to those in south Wales, which may even have been made by sculptors trained there. In some cases, individual patterns may occur in both places. For example, the pattern of a Cornish interlace cross at Cardinham, composed of four triquetra knots, is identical to those at Coychurch in South Glamorgan and Nevern in Dyfed. Also, the monasteries of St Buryan near Land's End and St Petroc at Bodmin appear to have had schools of sculptors like those identified in south Wales. In the Bodmin area, a series of crosses was set up around the monastery of St Petroc, which was flourishing in the tenth century. In the most notable of these, which stands at Cardinham, the sculptor used a variety of motifs, running spirals, ringloop interlace and a ring-chain that fades into a rectilinear meander pattern. The ring-chain is a motif the oldest known example of which is the cross at Michael, Isle of Man, which was carved by the tenth-century runemaster-sculptor Gaut Bjornsson.

As in other Celtic countries, stopping-places along paths, pilgrimage roads and trackways in Cornwall were marked by wayside crosses. The custom was maintained for many centuries, and as late as 1447 the Rector of the parish of Creed left money in his will to pay for the erection of new stone crosses in the county at stopping-places 'where dead bodies are rested on their way to burial, that prayers be made, and the bearers take some rest.' Churchyard crosses dating from the ninth and tenth centuries were often located to the right of the church entrance, and, as in the rest of northern Europe, there was a tradition of erecting crosses in market-places. Two tenth-century wheel-head crosses stand in Sancreed churchyard, both with representations of the crucifixion at the centre of the wheel-head. One bears the name Runhol, whose name is also discernible on a cross that stands near the door of Lanherne Convent. Formerly, this cross was in the parish of Gwinear, but, as is the case with so many crosses, it was moved.

The remains of a royal cross stand near the road to Liskeard about 1.6 km (1 mile) northwest of St Cleer. Reduced by breakage to part of a cross-shaft, the remains bear an inscription commemorating Doniert, who was King of Cornwall around the year 875. Close to the celebrated 'lost church' of St Piran at Perranporth stands a cross that is mentioned in a charter dating from the year 960. Unlike the majority of Celtic Crosses, it has pecked ornament rather than interlace or key-patterns. Its most notable feature, however, shows it to be a direct continuation of the older Pagan wheel-headed stones of the Celts, for its wheel-head is not a vertical Christian cross but an X-shape, with the four holes cut on the vertical and horizontal axes. Thus, it can be said that, technically, this ancient stone is not a cross at all but an instance of the older, Pagan, tradition of the continental Celts.

The crosses of the Isles of Scilly closely resemble those in Cornwall. Three ancient shaped granite crosses exist within the oval churchyard at St Buryan, originally an Irish settlement, while at St Mary's an old high cross serves as a gable cross on the church at Old Town. Two crosses once stood as boundary-markers on the site of the present St Mary's airport, and one of them, from High Cross Lane, Salakee, was removed in 1887 to St Mary's Church. During the nineteenth century, many of the crosses of the Isles of Scilly were taken away from their original positions by collectors. For example, in the nineteenth century, Mr E. N. V. Moyle, the Clerk to the Council of the Isles of Scilly, used his position of influence to assemble a notable collection of stones, including crosses, in his garden at Rocky Hill, St Mary's. It is arguable that the crosses were saved from destruction by their removal, but equally the disrespect for the sacred that allowed holy stones to be taken away for personal pleasure is a sign that a spiritual understanding of the landscape was already in decline.

The Anglo-Saxon Tradition

Around 2,500 pieces of Anglo-Saxon sculpture are known from England and southern Scotland. When they immigrated into Britain, the Angles and Saxons were Pagan, but they came under the influence of Celtic Christianity when Irish missionaries arrived to found monasteries in Wessex and Northumbria. Later, Roman Catholic missions came from the continent, and it was this influence which proved more lasting. In Northumbria, Benedict Biscop and Wilfrid brought in stonemasons and glaziers from Gaul and Rome to build churches and make artefacts, including, most probably, stone crosses. The designs on the earliest Northumbrian crosses have affinities with Egyptian and Syrian sources, and it is likely that their sculptors were trained outside the British Isles. The earliest of these Anglo-Saxon high crosses are at Bewcastle, Easby, Hexham, Otley and Ruthwell. They are all in the form of tapered cross-shafts sculpted with panels containing religious figures and ornament. The Bewcastle cross has a runic inscription that has been interpreted as being either a memorial to King Alcfrith or commemorating the Christianization of Cumbria by force of arms, around the year 670.

The fragments of a Northumbrian cross that commemorates Wilfrid's successor, Acca, can be seen at Hexham in Northumberland. According to the *Historia Regum* of the twelfth-century chronicler Symeon of Durham, Bishop Acca, who died in 740, was buried outside the east wall of Hexham Church. His grave was marked by two wonderfully carved crosses, one set up at the head and the other at the foot. They bore the inscription that Acca was buried there. The crosses were smashed at a later date, and only fragments were recovered. At the Reformation and in Cromwell's wars, most of the surviving Anglo-Saxon crosses suffered attacks from Protestant extremists, who, considering them to be symbols of 'Popery and superstition', smashed them with religious zeal. Even the best crosses did not escape. In the seventeenth century, one of the finest, at Ruthwell, was pulled down and broken up by activists following a Church of Scotland edict concerning 'idolatrous monuments in the kirk of Ruthwell'. Those we see today have been either re-erected or re-assembled from broken pieces.

The only Anglo-Saxon cross still retaining its original head is at Irton in Lancashire. It is similar in form to the Irish high crosses, but, in common with its Anglian counterparts, does not have a wheel-head. A fine full-sized replica of it can be seen in the Victoria and Albert Museum in

London. In addition to the Northumbrian school, there were separate schools of crossmaking in the other Anglian and Saxon kingdoms. The finest examples of Mercian crosses can be seen at Sandbach in Cheshire and at Bakewell and its environs. A school of cross-sculptors has been identified in Derbyshire at Bakewell, from which 65 examples, in various states of preservation, are known. Later Mercian crosses were refined into a form close to the classical Celtic wheel-head, by the addition of a ring.

Following Pagan practice, the Celtic church used mark-stones to sanctify crossing-places, such as fords and bridges and the entrances to holy enclosures. This practice was transmitted by Irish priests to the Anglo-Saxon church, through which it became part of the sacred landscape of England. Perhaps the most powerful instance of the cross as boundary-marker was at Beverley in Humberside (formerly Yorkshire), which in former times was one of the most holy places of England. The minster was given its rights in the year 937 by King Athelstan after he had borrowed the standard of St John of Beverley to use as his holy war-banner at the Battle of Brunanburgh where his greatly outnumbered English army defeated the combined forces of the Celto-Danish confederation. In the Beverley charter, Athelstan stated: 'In your church shall be a college of canons, endowed with ample possessions. It shall be a sanctuary, with a Frithstool before the altar, as a place of refuge and safety for debtors and criminals. Four stones, each a mile distant from this place, shall mark the bounds of the privileged ground. Your monastery shall be extended, and revenues increased, and the shrine of the Blessed John be amongst the most magnificent in the land.' King Athelstan was a promoter of the craft of masonry, which, as the masonic *Regius Poem* (*c.* 1400), tells us: 'came into England ... in the time of good King Athelstan's day.' Clearly, it was these masons who sculpted and erected Athelstan's stone crosses.

Standing stone crosses were the significant markers in Athelstan's geomantic layout of the Beverley sanctuary. Originally, the holy ground extended 2.5 km (1½ miles) in every direction from the Minster. The area within this was divided into a number of concentric enclosures of increasing sanctity, of which there were two main areas, one inside the other. The entry-points into the Outer and the Second at the north, east, south and west were marked by stone crosses, three of which still exist. The churchyard wall was the third boundary, inside which the western church door was the fourth. The next boundary-line came at the choir screen inside the church, and the sixth was the frithstool itself. This was a stone throne in which the fugitive from justice had to sit in order to claim sanctuary. Violators of the sanctuary were punished with an increasing scale of fines, beginning with the outer boundary with a fine of one Hundredth, being doubled at the next cross and so on as far as the frithstool in the inner sanctum. Violators of the frithstool itself, however, were declared outlaws and punished with death. Similar enclosures, marked by crosses at the four quarters, existed around holy places in Ireland, Scotland and Wales.

The Isle of Man

Situated between Britain and Ireland, and with a history of being first an independent Celtic island, then a Norse kingdom, the Isle of Man has its own unique crosses. As other Celtic countries, the earliest Manx crosses are inscribed standing stones, some of which bear inscriptions in ogham or Roman script. Some of these memorial stones are bilingual. One, at Knoc-y-doonee, Andreas, which dates from the sixth century, had on one face the Latin *Ammecat filius Rocat hic jacet* (Ambecatos son of Rocatos lies here), and on the left side the fragmental ogham Celtic inscription

(Am)b(e)catos maqi Rocatos. A standing stone from Maughold is interesting in being a transitional form from the standing memorial stone to the classical Celtic Cross. Inside a circle surrounded by an inscription in the manner of a seal is a hexafoli pattern that was the sigil of the goddess Juno in Roman religion. Beneath the Pagan goddess sigil are two *chi-rho* crosses with accompanying inscriptions.

The crosses of the Isle of Man developed in the same broad way as in other Celtic and Celtic-influenced areas. From the simple cross-inscribed standing stone developed the cross-slab with complex carvings, representing a standing cross amid ornament or mythic scenes. One of the most evocative Celtic crucifixion scenes is on a Manx stone of this type. Although it is a broken fragment, the remains of a late eighth-century slab from the Calf of Man depicts Christ on the cross, with Longinus about to spear him. Christ is richly dressed, with a roundel of interlace over his heart. Remarkable though this is, it is outside the mainstream of designs of Manx crosses. Another of the crosses at Maughold resembles Pictish examples, having a carving of a wheel-head cross, on either side of which is a seated monkish figure, representing Paul and Anthony, a popular theme in the Celtic church.

The 'boss' or 'serpent stone' style of the Pictish stones and the western Scottish and Irish crosses also appeared in the Isle of Man. At Maughold, Crux Guriat is a flat slab which has five bosses in a cross-pattern, carved just inside the ring of a wheel-head. The bosses, however, are in a much lower relief than those elsewhere and are not carved with the 'serpent's egg' interlace patterns. Furthermore, there is no actual cross within the circle. Unlike Crux Guriat, the Conchan crosses known by their prosaic catalogue numbers 92 and 93, are the forerunners of the free-standing stone crosses. Although they are slabs carved with crosses and beasts, it is likely that the tops of the stones were rounded to conform with the outline of the wheel-cross. In these two crosses, the wheel-head, cross and shaft are all composed of continuous interlace patterns, resembling nothing less than crosses composed entirely of wickerwork. Like others of this kind in Scotland, they give us the impression that the whole cross-slab is a picture of a free-standing cross in the land. Perhaps they represent wooden or wickerwork crosses that have not survived. The other Conchan cross (No. 74) is closer to the Irish tradition, where the cross-part and wheel-part are separated, as though the wheel is behind the cross as its support rather than integral with it. The form of cross where the stone has been shaped into a rounded form outlining the wheel, supported on a wide base like those at Llantwit Major and Margam, is also known in the Isle of Man, for example in a cross from Kirk Braddan and another at Lonan, which has the close, wickerlike interlace of the Conchan crosses. The next step in this development came when the cross 'escaped' entirely from the slab, and the freestanding stone Celtic Cross was born.

Under Norse rulership, which initially was Pagan, syncretic religious practices evolved, in which Christian and Pagan elements which had the same symbolic meaning co-existed alongside one another. Thus, Odin, Thor, Heimdall and other gods of the northern pantheon were carved by the Northmen. Also, the spirits of the land, rarely present in other Celtic crosses, the dwarfs, gnomes, trolls, giants and dragons, made their appearance on the Northmen's crosses in Man. These Manx crosses are important mythologically, for they depict several significant episodes from Norse sacred stories, including elements recognizable from the Pagan scriptures known as *The Edda*. Episodes from the life of the hero Sigurd Fafnirsbane are depicted on a number of Manx crosses, most notably those from Jurby, Malew and Maughold. The broken cross from Jurby shows the hero Sigurd, Wagner's Siegfried, killing the dragon Fafnir. Another cross from Jurby shows the

Rainbow Bridge, Bifröst, with Heimdall the warder of Asgard sounding the Gjallarhorn to summon all the gods to battle against the forces of destruction. On a cross thought to be the memorial of King Olaf the Red, who was killed at Ramsey in 1153, are depictions of the story of the trickster-god Loki. The Kirk Bride cross depicts the four dwarfs that hold up the sky in Norse cosmology, Nordri, Ostri, Sudri and Vestri; a figure with a staff, perhaps Odin; Thor, fighting the World Serpent; and the giant Gungnir. On a slab from Andreas, we can see Odin in combat with the Fenris-Wolf. Like the Cumbrian Gosforth Cross, the Manx crosses of the Norse period are wonderful examples of 'dual faith' religious syncretism, where archetypal myths of different systems coexist in perfect harmony.

Eighth-century Anglian runes have been found on the remains of crosses at Maughold, spelling out the names Blagc-Mon and —gmon. Both crosses have an early form of the cross pattee inscribed inside a circle, with remains of the Greek letters *alpha* and *omega*. Other runic inscriptions on Manx crosses are in the later Scandinavian runes of the tenth to thirteenth centuries. A stone found at Kirk Maughold bears an invocation in thirteenth-century runes: 'Krist: Malaki and Patrick: Adamnan: But of all the sheep Iuan is the priest in Kurna valley.' Although this runic inscription appears to be in honour of a Christian priest, when we encounter runic invocations to the saints it was not necessarily Christians who carved them. The process of making saints in the church is identical to the apotheosis of Pagan heroes who enter the pantheon to become divine, in the manner of Hercules or Alexander the Great. It is only according to the theological doctrine of the Christian religion that they do not become gods. Yet, like their Pagan counterparts, they also enter the otherworldly realms, from which they may be invoked to grant aid to human beings. Recognizing this, the Pagan Danes in Ireland invoked St Patrick as the god of the land in their struggles against the Norwegians there. As recorded in the Irish *Annals* of Mac Firbis: 'This St Patrick, against whom these enemies of ours have committed many evils, is archbishop and head of the saints of Erin. Let us pray to him fervently and let us give alms to him honourably for gaining victory and triumph over our enemies.'

Outside the British Isles

The Celtic Cross form is not unknown outside the British Isles, though its connection with the Celts may be tenuous or fortuitous, for occurrences are few and far between. In the late medieval period, small wayside crosses with wheel-heads about 1 metre (3 ft) in diameter were erected in parts of Germany. Also, in southwestern France and northern Spain, the traditional Basque tombstones, known as *estela discoidea*, include wheel-crosses as well as eight-fold wheels and hexagrams. Perhaps more closely related to the authentic Celtic tradition was an intriguing cross illustrated by the Danish antiquary Ole Worm in 1651 in Book Six of his *Danicorum Monumentorum*. This stone cross stood at Julskovkorset on the island of Fünen. It was in the form of a wheel-headed high cross that bore the inscription: 'In the year 1445 Wolfgang and his son Oluf had these letters chiselled.' A labyrinth was carved on the cross-shaft. Unfortunately, this remarkable high cross no longer exists. During the nineteenth century, the influence of the Celtic revival saw the erection of Celtic Crosses wherever there was British influence. In Brittany, a small British-style Celtic Cross was set up as a finial on the holy well at St Cado.

Chapter 9

IRISH HIGH CROSSES

The symbolic structure of the fully developed wheel-head Celtic Cross can be seen as representative of the *axis mundi* or cosmic axis. According to Welsh bardic traditions recorded in the middle ages, and taught by contemporary druidism, the cosmos is conceived as having several 'circles' or levels, which can be visualized as if they were stacked one on top of the other along an axis. Like *Irminsul*, this axis is the subtle link between the underworld below, through the middle earth on which we live, to the heavenly upperworld above. At birth, death and under some other special conditions during life, spirits migrate between these worlds. The Celtic Cross is conceived in terms of the bardic cosmic axis, which in contemporary psychological terms sees the base of the cross symbolizing the unconscious, the shaft the ascending consciousness, and the top transcendence.

The Cosmic Dimension

According to the Welsh spiritual tradition, the underworld is called Annwn, the middle world Abred, and the upper world Gwynvyd. A Welsh bardic text called *Y Tri Chyflwr* (The Three States) tells us: 'According to the three principal qualities of man shall be his migration in Abred; from laziness and mental blindness he shall fall to Annwn; from dissolute wantonness he shall traverse the circle of Abred, according to his necessity; and from his love for goodness he will ascend to the circle of Gwynvyd.' This idea is broadly in accord with the three Christian worlds of Hell, Earth and Heaven, though bardic tradition infers many journeys within the system through re-incarnation. These three worlds represent spiritual progress: 'The three states of living beings: Annwn, from which comes the beginning; Abred, in which knowledge increases, and hence goodness; and Gwynvyd, in which is the plenitude of goodness, knowledge, truth and endless life.'

Although the underworld is conceived as a place of the dead, it is not so much the infernal burning place of devilish torture of the Judaeo-Christian scriptures. Rather it resembles the Greek Hades as the gloomy abode of insubstantial shadows. Thus, itis called variously *affan*, the land invisible, *affwys*, the abyss, and *annwyn* or *annwfn*, the not-world. According to a bardic question-and-answer fragment, recorded in *Barddas*: '*Question*. In what place is Annwyn? *Answer*. Where there is the least possible of animation and life, and the greatest of death, without other condition.' Thus, the soil of the graveyard, in which the cross stands, is truly Annwn. Many high crosses are set on steps or a four-square pyramidal base, both of which are representations of the archetypal world mountain, inside which is the realm of the dead. The stepped bases or *perrons* recall the much more ancient step-pyramids and ziggurats of Egypt and Babylon whose terraces led upwards to a summit platform upon which the image of divinity was set. Powerful examples of stepped cross-bases exist at Llantwit Major and St David's in Wales, at Kildalton on Islay and Clackmannan in Scotland. Pagan forerunners of these cross-bases exist in Ireland at Mullaghmast in County Kildare and at Killycluggan in County Cavan. Classic examples of the four-square pyramidal cross-base exist in Ireland at

Ahenny, Castledermot and Monasterboice, while an intermediate form of stepped base supports St Martin's Cross on Iona. Their raised bases recall the earlier grave-mounds which were literally the abodes of the dead from which rose the axial memorial stone that pointed towards the heavens. According to Celtic folklore, these mounds are places where sensitive people can commune with the spirits of the departed. In his 1703 book *Gweledigaetheu y Bardd Cwsc*, Ellis Wynne describes three visions of this world, death and Hell, where the sleeping bard sees a vision of the dead, the Children of Annwn, dancing upon the churchyard mound. Celtic lore such as these reminds us that such mounds are not only places of burial but also places of vision, where one may glimpse the spirits of the otherworld.

Above the basal 'mound', the cosmic axis of the cross rises from the underworld into this world of living mortals, Abred. The axis leads ever upwards from middle earth to the heavenly upperworld, called in the bardic tradition The Circle of Gwynvyd, the 'White Land'. This is the bright realm represented as the wheel-cross, emblem of the sun above the earth as the symbol of the sky god, upon which the Christ is manifest. According to Breton beliefs, the cross of Christ is envisaged as a ladder from earth to heaven, down which God came to earth. By means of this divine ladder to heaven, human souls are enabled to climb to paradise. From the sixteenth century, when Breton priests began to re-consecrate prehistoric megaliths, it was customary to carve them with the symbols of the passion of Christ, which include a ladder.

Although crosses often end with the upper arm of the wheel-head, the most highly developed among them are topped by a little house which in bardic cosmology represents the heavenly throne or mansion of God, Ceugant. The most striking example is on top of Muiredach's Cross at Monasterboice. The capstone of the cross from Tihilly in County Offaly, preserved at University College in Dublin, is also house-shaped, as were probably the missing capstones of the crosses at Cloonfad and Duleek. The existing cross-top houses closely resemble known portable reliquaries, the small, highly decorated boxes in which holy relics, whether the bones of a saint, his book or some other sacred item, were kept. The *Annals of Ulster* tell of how the relics of Conlaed were placed in a shrine made of gold and silver, which coincides with the dating of Irish house-shrines from the eighth or ninth century. The *Annals of Clonmacnois* record that in 1129 among the relics stolen from the monastic altar was a reliquary in the form of a model of Solomon's Temple in Jerusalem, which in Judaeo-Christian tradition was the reflection of the heavenly mansion of God on Earth. The *Book of Kells* shows us the Irish idea of what the Jerusalem Temple looked like. It is depicted in a representation of the Temptation of Christ by the Devil. Christ is on the ridge of a steeply gabled roof which is covered with tiles or shingles and adorned with serpents'-head finials. The temple walls are similarly adorned with scales or ornamented panels.

A number of these jewelled miniature houses have come down to us through the centuries because of the excellent Celtic custom that relics are preserved by hereditary keepers. Among the finest are the Monymusk Reliquary in the National Museum of Scotland in Edinburgh, and the Emly Shrine. Dating from the year 800, the latter is kept in the Museum of Fine Arts in Boston, Massachusetts. Others, taken as booty by Viking raiders, and later buried with their new owners, re-emerged from archaeological excavations in recent times. The museums at Copenhagen and Trondheim house notable examples. They are all eloquent testimony to the exquisite artistry and craftsmanship of their makers.

Irish holy objects show a repetition of house shapes ranging from those large enough for a human being to enter to those small enough to hold in one hand. This repeating hierarchy is a classic instance of the Celtic concept of self-similarity. According to this hierarchical system, the unseen universal Mansion of God is the largest, within that the church, then the reliquary-tomb and finally, within it, the metal reliquary itself.

Several surviving ancient Irish churches show the prototype for the house-shrines. The pilgrimage church on St MacDara's Island in County Galway is one of the best examples, having been restored recently with its original roof-ornament of Y-shaped gable finials. The church at Killinaboy in County Clare bears a cross on its west end that recalls the reliquary of the True Cross once kept inside. Inside some churches were reliquary-tombs whose form reflected the churches in which they stood. Extant examples are the reliquary-tombs at Banagher in County Londonderry, Saul in County Down, Clones in County Monaghan and the Skull House at Cooley in County Donegal. They are all in the form of houses of the dead, the so-called 'mortuary houses'. The Clones mortuary house, which probably contained relics of St Tighernach, has gable finials, once stood inside a church, now destroyed. Inside such stone shrines, smaller wooden or metal ones may have been deposited. The small metal Lough Erne Shrine, actually demonstrates the principle of self-similarity by containing a small shrine within a larger one of the same form. The practice of carving a representation of the crucifixion upon a cross, where Christ is shown on another cross, is yet another instance of Celtic self-similarity.

Because, according to Christian cosmology, the souls of those who die blameless go to live in the heavenly house at the apex of the cosmos, the houses on top of Celtic crosses are an expression of this belief. It is not just a Christian concept, however, for it exists also in Nordic cosmology, where the house of the dead symbolizes the great hall of Odin, Valhalla. The flowering of the Irish high cross came after contact with the Pagan cosmology of the Northmen, for the house of the dead was an important element in Germanic and Norse belief. The Anglo-Saxon chronicler, Bede, recounts that the memorial of St Chad, who died in the year 670, was made of wood in the shape of a gabled house. Also, the two known wooden coffins of seventh-century Archbishops of Canterbury were also both in the form of the house of the dead: one had a hipped roof with a convex section, and the other had a high-pitched gabled roof.

The Anglo-Saxon Hedda Stone in Peterborough Cathedral is a more durable example of the Canterbury wooden coffins, being in the form of a carved stone house-tomb 1.5 metres (5 ft) in length. It has a roof sculpted with birds, beasts and interlace, while the walls below are arcaded with figures standing in each niche or doorway. These doors with guardian figures recall the Norse accounts of the many doorways of Valhalla. According to *The Edda*, from the 540 doors of the Allfather's hall come the dead, in the shape of the Einherjar, Odin's heroes, to fight against the powers of evil and destruction. Unfortunately, a few years ago, during building works in the cathedral, the Hedda stone was handled carelessly and damaged by having parts broken off it. The cast in the Victoria and Albert Museum shows the condition of the stone before this incident. Another important surviving house-shrine tomb is the Kentish Fordwich stone, which is believed to have originated in Canterbury. About the same length as the Hedda Stone, it is in the form of a building with a slightly curving pitched roof, carved with 'beaver-tail' tiles, and with walls sculpted as an arcade in the Romanesque manner.

In parts of England and southern Scotland are a number of recumbent stone grave-markers known by the generic term of 'hogsback tombstones'. Associated mainly with areas of Norse settlement, they are made in the form of a Scandinavian house of the time, generally boat-shaped with flattened ends like a Cambridge punt. Although it is possible that they recall ship-burials, their form is primarily the 'house of the dead'. The form of these houses of the dead is taken from the Nordic timber-framed houses whose frame structure was based upon the cruck principle rather than the box-frame. Hogsbacks are a direct development of the pagan *omphalos*-shaped bauta-stones that were erected on grave-mounds. These houses are depicted as having a tiled roof, whose ridge is sometimes the spine of a dragon or a serpent, resembling the coffins of the Alamanni, which were carved from tree-trunks. Beneath the roof are the walls, which in some cases bear interlace patterns, and in others, warriors. There is a Nordic folk tradition that the walls of the house of the dead were woven from snakes, and its form also resembles the wickerwork coffins used in former times in some areas. A hogsback, formerly at the old Anglian royal place of Repton in Derbyshire, had spiralling serpents carved on its walls. Unfortunately, it was broken up early in the nineteenth century.

A hogsback in Durham Cathedral Library has its ends protected by bears with bands around their muzzles, grasping and supporting the roof-ridge of the house. Almost identical houses of the dead are kept in the church at Brompton in North Yorkshire, where there were once ten such examples. Similar bear-stones are known from Lowther in Cumbria and Heysham in Lancashire. A fragment of hogsback from the Hospitium at York shows that its sides were composed of carved interlace and scrollwork, over which was a representation of a shingled roof. The churchyard at Penrith in Cumbria contains four such tiled-roof stones, and there are similar ones at Deerness in Orkney and St Boniface's churchyard on Papa Westray. A stone of this type from Falstone in Northumberland has a double inscription in Anglo-Saxon and runic letters on the walls, which are scribed into parallel lines like wooden boards. Other fine examples exist at Sockburn in County Durham and Govan in Glasgow. One of the Govan stones is in the form of a beast, where the roof-tiles are interpreted as scales, while another has a serpent as the roof-ridge, with the tile-pattern appearing as many small doors, recalling those of Valhalla. It is clear from all of these British instances that both the Celtic reliquaries and the Nordic houses of the dead are part of the same tradition as the houses carved on top of the Irish high crosses.

The High Crosses of Ireland

The Celtic Cross attained its most refined form in Ireland in the shape of the high cross, and we are fortunate that the ravages of Puritan zealots were less thorough there than in Great Britain. Many excellent ancient crosses survive, some even in their original locations. Only their colour is lost, and, with the effects of time and weather, some of them are eroded. Nevertheless, they provide wonderful examples of the high level of skill and artistry of their makers. However, we should not lose sight of the fact that many ancient crosses have been destroyed, and those that remain are only part of the story of the Celtic Cross.

Stylistically, seven classes have been identified by commentators, but, surprisingly, there are no high crosses in the south and west of Ireland. The first class of high cross is the Ahenny group. The two fine crosses at Ahenny in Tipperary are considered to be the earliest existing examples of Irish free-standing wheel-head crosses. Dating from some time soon after the year 700, they have relatively little figurative sculpture. At Ahenny, the South Cross is carved with spirals and interlace. There are also five bosses, one for each of the arms of the cross, and one marking the centre. On top of both of the Ahenny crosses are tapering cylindrical caps that resemble the tops of some Slavonic Pagan pillar-stones. Another notable cross of the Ahenny kind is at Kiltieran.

The second class is the Bealin Group. Named after the cross-fragment at Bealin in Westmeath, which has a round, shieldlike centre, this group includes the North Cross at Clonmacnois. Dating from the late eighth or early ninth centuries, these crosses have interlace and spiral ornament, and some images of horsemen. The third group includes the crosses at Castledermot, Moone and Old Kilcullen, all in County Kildare. Like those of the Bealin Group, they date from the late eighth or the early ninth centuries. They are good examples of the playful way that the crossmakers used mixed motifs with classical Celtic inventiveness. The eastern sides of the two crosses at Castledermot have crucifixion scenes at the centre of the wheel-head, for it is customary for the crucifixions depicted on Celtic Crosses to face towards the east. The South Cross at Castledermot mixes panels depicting human scenes with interlace and spirals. The east face has human panels, while the west is interlace. There is a notable depiction of the patron of monks, St Anthony of Egypt, in combat with beastly demons. The underworldly base of this cross has the usual hunting scenes common elsewhere.

The Celtic Cross at Moone is over 5 m (16½ ft) high and is set upon a tapering base surmounted by a pyramidal crown that in turn supports the shaft. This cross is believed to be the earliest that has a coherent scheme of decoration where episodes from the Old Testament and New Testament are arranged thematically. The basal stone is carved with various figures. The eastern front bears 12 figures, assumed to be the 12 apostles that were a popular theme for French Christians to carve on megaliths. Just below the cross top on the eastern side, a panel in the shape of an Egyptian Diamond contains a figure that may be interpreted as the risen Christ. The centre of the cross does not have a crucifixion scene, but spirals. On the opposite, western side, there is a crucifixion scene, but again this is placed beneath the cross and not at its centre.

Made of granite quarried at Castledermot, the cross at Moone was lost for centuries, having been broken and the fragments buried. It was rediscovered shortly after the Potato Famine, when the local stone-mason, Michael O'Shaughnessy, unearthed its base and head while collecting pieces of stone from the ruined abbey for new buildings. The cross-fragments were recovered, and the head was set up on the base. Later, during grave-digging, a part of the shaft was excavated. In 1893, three of O'Shaughnessy's sons reassembled the three parts, but with some of the shaft still missing. So it stands today.

At Kells in the county of Meath are four crosses that remain in various stages of integrity. They form the fourth group of Irish Celtic Crosses. Three stand within the church precincts, and the fourth stands in the middle of the road at the centre of the town as a market cross. One of the churchyard crosses is broken and incomplete, while another, perhaps the most interesting of the four crosses, is unfinished. This 'Unfinished Cross' was assembled in the nineteenth century from some cross-components that had for some reason been abandoned before finishing. Because of this fortunate accident of fate, we can see the way that the stonemason carved the basic form to allow the laying-out of interlace and figure patterns. The other three crosses were finished, and contain a wealth of figure sculpture of Biblical and other scenes that include some remarkable symbolism. The Broken Cross has a scene of the Baptism of Christ, in which the River Jordan is shown as a confluence of streams coming from two circular wells, reflecting the Celtic veneration of sources of rivers such as the Seine, Shannon and Severn. The South Cross at Kells also contains an image that is a clear continuation of Pagan tradition. At the centre of the wheel-head is an image of Christ in the posture of the Egyptian god Osiris, who was slain and resurrected like Jesus. The Osiris-Christ holds a cross and a blooming bough that alludes to the legendary golden bough and silver branch of Druidism. The market cross is notable for its scenes of the Celtic martial arts, including wrestling and quarter-staff fighting.

The fifth class of Irish high crosses is characterized by the now-destroyed Cross of Armagh, formerly at the headquarters of the archbishops of Ireland. Now only a few pieces remain, but its former glory is recorded in old engravings which show that the cross was covered with Biblical episodes arranged in a strictly logical order. The cross at Arboe in County Tyrone is the best surviving example of this rigorous arrangement.

The sixth group includes crosses at Clonmacnois, Monasterboice and Durrow. Clonmacnois in County Offaly preserves a fine collection of Celtic carvings. It is renowned for its grave-slabs, carved with Celtic crosses, names and invocations in ancient script. There are also a number of ancient crosses at Clonmacnois. A fragment of headless cross-shaft that exists to the north of the old church bears a carving of the horned god of the forest, Cernunnos, who in Brittany was worshipped as St Hoeirnin. Often, far from being destroyed by Christian priests, images of the old gods were maintained at the shrines where once they were the chief deities. St Fergus's cemetery on the island of Innishkeen in Upper Loch Erne still preserves the antlered stone head of a Celtic divinity. This Clonmacnois cross dates from around the year 800. The South Cross at Clonmacnois is a little more recent, dating from around 825. It is mostly carved with interlace and bosses, with a crucifixion on the westward side.

Considered to be one of the finest Celtic Crosses in Ireland is Flann's Cross. Named after King Flann, it is also called The Cross of the Scriptures. It stands to the west of the enclosure at Clonmacnois. A mutilated inscription at the bottom of the cross-shaft commemorates Flann, who died in the year 916, and Abbot Colman, who died in 921. Above the inscription is a carving of the king and abbot setting up a post, which may represent a cross. The centre of the wheel-cross has an image of Christ enthroned in the Osirian position. The ring of this cross is emphasized. Instead of the usual method of construction, in which the stonemasons made a cross and attached four arcs of stone to make the wheel, the designer of this cross emphasized the wheel in the form of a continuous stone ring linking four roundels. Thus, the centre cross with Christ in majesty is separated from the arms of the cross outside the ring. On top of the cross is a carving of a house-shrine.

At Monasterboice in County Louth are two more fine Celtic Crosses, both of which are intact and on their original sites. The West Cross, which measures 6.7 m (22 ft) is the highest ancient cross remaining in Ireland. The cross-shaft is carved with panels that represent scenes from Biblical mythology. The wheel-head of the West Cross, which contains a number of bosses, is in a better state of preservation than the shaft or the house-shrine cap. It is likely that the cross was repaired in antiquity with new stone that replaced the original, for the depiction of the crucified Christ, whose head lolls to one side, is in the manner of later styles.

The other, more famous, cross at Monasterboice (illustrated on page 84), is that of Muiredach, named after the Abbot who died in the year 922. He is commemorated by an inscription at the base of the shaft on the west side. The cross measures 5.5 m (18 ft), though some of the lower part of the shaft is missing now, the cross having been re-erected on its original pyramidal base. This cross is a remarkable synopsis of syncretic religion. Its east and west faces are sculpted with Biblical scenes, while the sides have spirals, bosses with interlace, and intertwining beasts. The outer part of the wheel-head is carved with bands of interlace between which are intertwining serpents. At the centre of the east face is an image of Christ, based on the iconography of the resurrected Egyptian god, Osiris. Christ is holding a cross and *Irminsul*-staff in the Osirian position, and on his head is an eagle that resembles the crown of Egyptian gods and pharaohs. On the left of Christ is the Great God Pan with his pipes, while on the right is a harp-playing figure, who is King David or Apollo. The tension between the emotional left side, and the rational right side is resolved in the figure of Christ, the perfect man.

The seventh and final grouping of high crosses arose in Ireland during the eleventh century, perhaps in County Clare, where a school of crossmakers operated from the late eleventh to the mid-twelfth centuries. There are six known crosses in this style at Kilfenora, three of which have sculpted figures. The Doorty Cross here has complex animal interlace. In comparison with the 'scriptural' high crosses, the figure sculpture of this school has been increased in size, the crucifixion is more prominent, interlace is reduced or absent and ring-heads, where present, are no longer pierced or drilled through. There are cross-fragments in this style in the churchyard at Killeany in the Aran Islands, but the most famous example stands at Dysert O'Dea. Although the pyramidal base of earlier crosses is retained, along with a pyramidal capstone, the mason created a cross-head without a ring, but with knobs in place of the customary holes. With a relatively large Christ figure, the cross effectively became a crucifix. Beneath Christ, the customary scenes from Biblical episodes are no longer present; instead, a medieval bishop, complete with mitre and spiral-headed crozier, stands guard. Crosses of this period are relatively localized to the west and south midlands of Ireland. They are known from Cashel, Drumcliff, Inishcaltra, Mona Incha, Roscrea, Sligo and Tuam. There is only one exception, at Glendalough, in the east of Ireland.

Scottish High Crosses

Outside Ireland, the Celtic Crosses on the holy island of Iona and at Kildalton on Islay in Strathclyde are closest in design to the Irish high crosses. The ninth-century cross in the churchyard at Kildalton is the most impressive surviving wheel-head Celtic Cross outside Ireland. Measuring 2.7 metres (9 ft) in height, the whole cross was carved from one piece of stone. It has a few bosses and serpents, but these are subordinate to spirals, interlace and panels containing episodes from the Old Testament. According to a 1982 survey of Iona by experts from the Royal Commission on the Ancient and Historical Monuments of Scotland, St John's, St Martin's and St Oran's crosses were made during the second half of the eighth century. St Matthew's Cross, of which only a fragment still exists, dates from the late ninth or early tenth centuries. It has been suggested that St John's Cross was made originally without a wheel-head, and that, because it was weak, had the ring added later to strengthen it. Made of stone imported from Argyll, it had one of the widest spans of any cross known in the British Isles. Its original base now supports a replica.

Like St John's Cross and that at Kildalton, the Ionan cross of St Martin is a fine example of the 'boss style', carved with masterly skill. The arms of this cross have slots at the end which may have held metal or wooden pieces, perhaps for the suspension of garlands, ribbons or banners. The 'serpent stone' bosses on St Martin's Cross resemble those on the Dunfallandy cross-slab in Tayside, and the Irish high crosses at Ahenny and the South Cross at Clonmacnois. Although commentators have suggested that they are derived from metalworking, they and their metal counterparts resemble the rope knotwork used in sailing ships and practised today by canal-boat enthusiasts. The astonishing Celtic knotwork plug for the font in the church at Kilpeck in Hereford and Worcester is another parallel which is often overlooked. The creation of Celtic high crosses continued on Iona long after they had passed into the 'gothic' style elsewhere. Later high crosses, such as the fifteenth-century MacLean's Cross on Iona, are rather simple when compared with the scriptural crosses of Ireland and Islay. Later medieval high crosses, such as MacMillan's Cross at Kilmorie in Knapdale, retain the circular portion of the wheel-head but no longer have the wheel form. Instead, at Kilmorie, there is a crucifixion scene, and the lower part bears a sword flanked by simple interlace carving.

Chapter 10

THE FALL AND RISE OF THE CELTIC CROSS

The advent of the Gothic art style led to the end of the Celtic high cross. In prosperous places, more ornate architectural styles were favoured, and high crosses were superseded. In remote, poorer areas, such as the Highlands and Islands of Scotland, the Celtic high cross was simplified, eventually losing its main characteristics. However, although the ornate high crosses were no longer made, the tradition of Celtic interlace art did not die out, but was maintained throughout the middle ages by craftspeople in Ireland, parts of Wales and the west Highlands of Scotland. Appropriately, the holy island of Iona remained a significant centre of the tradition. The medieval sculptors who carved grave-slabs in the west Highlands re-interpreted the traditional interlace patterns once used on high crosses in combination with contemporary artistic styles. In Ireland and Wales, too, the knowledge of the art did not die out, but adapted itself according to the tastes of the time.

Continuity and Destruction

There are a number of surviving late medieval artefacts that demonstrate the continuation of traditional Celtic art. A notable Irish example is the fifteenth-century leather satchel made as a container for *The Book of Armagh*. Kept in Trinity College, Dublin, it is stamped with patterns that reflect the full repertoire of Celtic ribbonwork and animal interlaces. The famous ivory and metal Eglinton Casket (on show in the National Museum of Antiquities in Edinburgh), once thought to date from the first millennium, appears to be one of the finest products of the west Highlands in the early sixteenth century. The brass ring brooch from Tomintoul, Grampian, illustrated here, dates from the seventeenth century and contains wonderful four-and five-fold knotwork roundels. This so-called 'revival' demonstrates that the principles of Celtic interlace were understood and used by traditional craftspeople in Scotland well into the eighteenth century. It seems that the catastrophes of the Jacobite rebellions and the subsequent repression of Highland culture after 1746 led to the suspension of Celtic art in Scotland for a period, but not to its permanent suppression.

At the Reformation, places and things formerly revered by Roman Catholics as holy were condemned by the new Protestants as objects of superstition that should be destroyed. In those parts of the British Isles where staunch Protestants gained the ascendancy, most of the crosses were destroyed in the religious turmoil that marked the change from Catholicism. Puritan zealots believed it to be their religious duty to eliminate all 'idolatrous images' at which Catholic 'superstition' was practised. So, when they smashed and burnt the church's images of Christ, Our Lady and the saints, broke stained-glass windows and dug up altars, they also destroyed stone crosses both on church ground and at the wayside. An English law against witchcraft, passed in 1542, specifically mentions the latter practice, in the shape of certain people who had 'digged up and pulled down an infinite number of crosses within this realm, for despite of Christ, or for love of money'.

It was the Puritan destroyers, however, who by their

activism had led the way in smashing churches. Because of their activities, those who believed treasure to lie beneath crosses could dig without fear of divine vengeance. However, the law did not recognize this, and condemned cross-destroyers as anti-Christian witches, or alternatively as people who believed the widespread story that treasure could be discovered beneath crosses. Because the Protestants wrecked so many churches and crosses without divine vengenace descending upon them, it became apparent to everyone that anyone could vandalize or loot a church or dig up a cross without fear of God's summary punishment. Then destruction could proceed without hindrance. In Scotland, the Edinburgh Parliament authorized the destruction of sacred places in 1581 with an act that stated: 'the Dregs of Idolatry yet remain in divers Parts of the Realm by using of Pilgrimage to some Chapels, Wells, Crosses, and such other Monuments of Idolatry, as also by observing the Festal days of the Saints sometime Named their Patrons in setting forth of Bon-Fires, singing of Carols within and about Kirks at certain Seasons of the Year.' This act to extirpate folk piety was the authorization by which many Scottish crosses were cast down and smashed. A thousand years of tradition was broken at a stroke.

So, outside Ireland and South Uist, which remained largely Catholic, the crosses were destroyed wholesale. As stone is a useful material, however, the pieces were not always thrown away, but re-used for other, profane, purposes. Fine crosses were broken up for their stone to be re-used as building material in houses, or as roadstone and gateposts. In some places, no use could be found for the crosses, so the fragments were buried or otherwise removed from sight. The scale of destruction was enormous. Before the Reformation, every churchyard had at least one cross; there were numerous wayside stopping-places marked by crosses, and every market-place had its market cross. Places of great sanctity had many crosses, and the oral tradition of

Iona recalls that over 200 crosses from there and the islands nearby were tossed into the sea by fanatics.

Rediscovery of the Celtic Heritage

This wholesale destruction of sacred artefacts had an effect on art styles. After the Puritan iconoclasm, Celtic interlace was no longer seen as an everyday part of life by all those who passed the local cross. It became a misty memory, whose nature was misunderstood and unrecognized. Thus, in learned circles, most understanding of the principles of Celtic art was lost, though in certain craft circles the knowledge was maintained among initiates. Also, especially in Ireland, knowledge of other esoteric Celtic traditions was maintained by local bards, wise women and cunning men. Knowledge and use of the ogham script continued among the people, being used occasionally on tombstones until the present day. In the nineteenth century at Kinsale in County Cork lived a man named Collins who had a poem about the zodiac painted on his walking-stick in white ogham characters. His cart also bore his name in ogham, and he was prosecuted for not writing it in the Roman alphabet.

Even where Celtic art was not completely ignored, learned artists from the academies contented themselves with copying earlier examples as instances of ancient barbarism rather than high art with a contemporary value. Unfortunately, because they did not take care to work according to the proper principles, what they produced was of inferior quality, and often broke the simplest rules, such as those for constructing basic interlace patterns. Even those artists who worked with antiquaries to record the remains of ancient Celtic art often drew impressions of what they saw, rather than accurate detail. Camden's *Britannia*, the first great attempt to document British antiquities, contains illustrations that were insufficiently accurate for later scientific archaeologists. However, it is only through the prodigious work of these early antiquaries that we know anything about many ancient crosses and other monuments. Another stalwart recorder of ancient monuments was the Oswestry scholar Edward Lhuyd (1660-1709), sometime keeper of the Ashmolean Museum in Oxford, who wrote about many Welsh antiquities that subsequently have been lost or destroyed.

It was not in Wales, however, that the fortunes of Celtic art first took a turn for the better, but in Scotland and Ireland. Scottish national romanticism, promoted by Sir Walter Scott and given considerable impetus by George IV's visit to Edinburgh in 1822, led to the revival of highland dress and the resumption of production of Celtic jewellery, based on surviving examples. Writing in *The British Architect* in 1875, notable Neo-Gothic architect William Burges recognized Scott's seminal role, stating that '... the real restorer of medieval art was Sir Walter Scott'. After Scott's impetus, the restored tradition was reinforced later by Queen Victoria's patronage, which ultimately resulted in a return to the manufacture of Celtic Crosses in stone, mainly as graveyard memorials. Commentators on Celtic art often condemn this period as being a conscious revival that has no artistic or spiritual value. However, this attitude is often conditioned by the political theory that tradition has no place in the modern world. Nineteenth-century Celtic Crosses stand as authentic products of the Celtic spirit, however removed some of the individual pieces may be from the traditional current.

The general revival in Christian art in the United Kingdom under Queen Victoria, which at that time included the whole of Ireland, provided the impetus for proper study of ancient ecclesiastical art. Of course, the Celtic Cross was recognized then as one of the most notable instances of early Christian art in the British Isles. An interest in crosses in general was expressed by the publication in 1875 of

Alfred Rimmer's *The Ancient Stone Crosses of England* (Virtue and Co.) Again, in this book, because of a lack of understanding of the principles, the illustration of Celtic interlace and key-patterns was poor, as in an engraving of the Nevern cross, which completely fails to depict the ornament correctly. However, Rimmer did express the general feeling of loss; that the sacred landscape had been destroyed wantonly by Puritan vandalism. 'Could road-side crosses have remained to the present day', wrote Rimmer, 'they would have been cherished objects in almost every village in England.'

Because of the dedicated work of antiquaries over the years, gradually a general awareness grew that the past mattered. Then, those old stone crosses that had been abandoned and used as bridges over streams, as building blocks or as gateposts to fields were located and removed to museums. In 1892, the antiquary Archdeacon Griffiths of Carmarthen donated an early Christian monument to the Cardiff Free Library and Museum. The process then began of taking away stone crosses from their original sites and displaying them in national museums in London, Cardiff, Edinburgh and Dublin. However, there was an alternative to the wholesale removal of monuments from their proper location. In the 1860s, the London firm of Brucciani and Company was established as the most able producer of plaster casts of antique monuments. The non-destructive technique used by Brucciani involved covering the stones with gelatine sheet and materials through which moisture could not penetrate. Then the clay and plaster used for the process of casting did not come into contact with the valuable carvings, yet reproduced them faithfully. This technique was used with ancient sculptures from Greece and Rome, and substantial collections of them still exist, most notably at the Museum of Classical Archaeology at Cambridge.

During the 1890s, a collection of Welsh crosses was begun by the curator of the Cardiff Free Library and Museum, which served as the basis for the present collection of crosses in the National Museum of Wales. In 1894, using Brucciani's technique, a programme was set up to make and collect casts of ancient stones, beginning with the famous crosses and slabs from Margam and Bridgend. W. Clarke of Llandaff took over the task from Brucciani in 1900, and continued with the programme of making casts of all known stones. Being from Wales, Clarke's brief was expanded to look for any 'as yet undiscovered or forgotten', and, gradually, as in other parts of the British Isles, a comprehensive knowledge was built up. Casts of crosses from other parts of the British Isles were made at the same time, and some of these replicas can be seen in the Victoria and Albert Museum in London and the National Museum of Ireland in Dublin. Ironically, subsequent degradation of the real stones as the result of air pollution means that many of these replicas now show more detail than the originals.

Towards the end of the nineteenth century, antiquaries and archaeologists began to make systematic studies of the Celtic Crosses of their respective localities. In his *Old Cornish Crosses*, published in 1896, A. G. Langdon recorded 360 examples from that county alone, which made Rimmer's earlier estimate of 5,000 crosses in England appear rather conservative. The antiquary J. Romilly Allen (1847–1907) also took an academic approach to Celtic monuments, recording them accurately with measured drawings. It was Romilly Allen who laid the foundations for the current resurgence of Celtic art. His book, *The Early Christian Monuments of Scotland* (The Pinkfoot Press), published at Edinburgh in 1903, was followed by works on Wales and *Celtic Culture in Pagan and Pre-Christian Times* (1904). The results of the new science of archaeology were significant in the restoration of Celtic art that we see today. Nineteenth-century Romantic artists like William Hole integrated all sorts of Celtic archaeological artefacts from different places and periods into their historic paintings.

Yet, despite their historical inaccuracy, there is no dissonance. Such paintings work as art, attesting to the underlying spirit of Celtic tradition.

At this time, as the result of a renewed interest in vernacular tradition, Celtic art assumed an important part in the repertoire of the Arts-and-Crafts movement. Based upon indigenous principles, it took traditional design elements and reinterpreted them in a modern form. Located at Compton, near Guildford in Surrey, the Watts Mortuary Chapel is one of the most remarkable Celtic Arts-and-Crafts buildings ever erected. Designed by Mary Fraser-Tytler Watts, wife of the eminent Victorian painter George Frederick Watts, it incorporates Celtic Crosses unlike any seen before, yet completely within the tradition. Each and every part of Mary Watts's chapel contains a symbolic meaning, reflecting her saying 'All creation is the garment of God'. Constructed of brick and terracotta, it is a masterly design of such stunning originality that makes it all the more regrettable that she spent her life in the shadow of 'England's Michelangelo' rather than practising in her own right as an architect. In keeping with the spiritual ethos of the Arts-and-Crafts movement, that local materials and techniques should be used as far as possible, she set up a pottery using local clay to make the terracotta panels, roundels and other decorative elements of the chapel. This pottery, which continued to produce wares until the 1950s, also made terracotta tombstones of various designs of Celtic Crosses, many of which can be seen in the graveyard in which the chapel is set. The chapel's symbolic decoration includes a number of roundels that progressively denote spiritual evolution in addition to the Celtic Cross illustrated here. Like ancient Celtic Crosses, the Watts chapel is truly part of the land, for it is made of materials won from the local earth, related perfectly to its location in the landscape.

On the Isle of Man, the Arts-and-Crafts architect Baillie Scott used the Celtic Cross in the ornament of some of his houses. For example, in Onchan, he built the houses Breaside and Leafield, and ornamented them with wheel-crosses made of pebbles standing proud of the cement rendering of the external walls. At Glen Falcon, built three years later in 1900, he made a copper fireplace-surround with a repoussé pattern of an eight-fold cross in Manx tradition. Ornamental elements from Celtic Crosses were popularized by the Manx designer Archibald Knox in his metal-work for Liberty and Company. In Ireland the Arts-and-Crafts-inspired Dun Emer Guild, founded by Evelyn Gleeson in 1902, produced textiles and carpets that used Celtic Cross interlace and tesselation patterns. Later, the foundation of the Irish Free State in 1921 gave impetus to the promotion of Celtic art as a national style. It has held its position since then.

However, Ireland's troubles also led to one of the worst losses of ancient Celtic manuscripts. This took place in June 1922 during the Irish Civil War, when the Four Courts in Dublin, held by Republican soldiers, was shelled by Free State artillery. The building, used by the Irish Republican Army as a munitions store, received a direct hit from a shell and exploded catastrophically. The Irish National Archive, held in the building and containing many priceless documents, was totally destroyed in one blow. After the victory of the Free State faction, however, Celtic monuments were erected to those who fell in the war. In the United Kingdom, too, to commemorate 'The Great War for Civilisation', the Celtic Cross was adopted as the model for many of the numerous war memorials that were erected in almost every village to honour those who had died in the conflict. Wherever possible, the new British war memorials were erected at places where crosses had stood in former times. Thus, stone crosses were restored to the British landscape as new representatives of the 'cherished objects' whose loss Rimmer had lamented 50 years earlier.

In the 1920s, interest in Celtic artwork continued. In 1922, the English fantasy artist Sidney Sime designed a cover for the libretto of Josef Holbrooke's opera, *Bronwen*. It showed the hero and heroine standing beneath a Pictish-type cross-slab with interlace panels in the form of a swastika. Of course, before the 1930s, that ancient sign had none of the bad connotations later attached to it by the Nazis. As an ancient symbol for lightning, it appears on ancient slabs like the Craignarget Stone, and occasionally upon graveyard memorials like Professor Cecil Bendall's Celtic Cross in Cambridge, which refers to his Hindu connections. Following the work of earlier antiquaries, especially Romilly Allen, from the 1920s, the Scottish artist George Bain investigated actual examples of Celtic art from Pictish stones and Celtic manuscripts, and, by analysis, expanded on Romilly Allen's re-discoveries. George Bain's main intention was to bring Celtic art back into the repertoire of contemporary artists, craftspeople and designers. His master-work, *Celtic Art: The Methods of Construction* (McLellan), first published in 1951, which contains his analysis, of the principles underlying Celtic art, has become the standard work on Celtic art. As Bain intended, the book became the greatest influence on contemporary Celtic artists, and remains so today.

Through the work of Romilly Allen, George Bain and his son Iain, and the Irish artist John G. Merne, the principles of Celtic art are understood once more, and there has been a renaissance of Celtic art in every field except, paradoxically, that of making stone crosses. The Celtic artists Jim Fitzpatrick, Courtney Davis, David James and Simon Rouse are among the most notable contemporary exponents of the style in book illustrations, posters and paintings, often with a spiritual content. Fantasy artists, illustrating the works of J. R. R. Tolkien and his imitators, have taken to Celtic art as the authentic reflection of the elder times in northern Europe. Similarly, with a recognition of ancestral tradition, contemporary jewellers are now making Celtic

Crosses of precious metals as pendants to wear around the neck, and small replicas of Celtic Crosses are available as ornaments. Since the 1980s, elements of Celtic art have become a significant current in the repertoire of the tattooist. Celtic Crosses, interlace and stylized animal patterns adorn the human body. This art is worldwide. Among the most notable contemporary tattooists putting Celtic Crosses on people are Darren Rosa and Jonathan Shaw of New York, Geoff Wilson of Lillydale, Australia, and 'Crazy Greg' of Heidelberg, Germany. Their work is in some way a contemporary restoration of the body art of the ancient Picts and Copts.

In 1996, the continuing awareness of the Celtic Cross was evidenced by the British Royal Mint issuing of a £1 coin, designed by Norman Sillman. Its reverse ('tails') side bears a Celtic Cross, representative of Northern Ireland. However, a revival of making new, full-sized, coloured Celtic Crosses is still awaited. All of the appropriate knowledge and skills exist among contemporary practitioners of Celtic art, and this is ample evidence that the Celtic tradition, already 2,700 years old, will continue to flourish in the foreseeable future.

GAZETTEER

There are a large number of crosses and related stones remaining in the Celtic realms. It is not possible to list them all, nor are all of them accessible. Also, like everything in the landscape, crosses are subject to destruction, either through accident, neglect or unthinking development, like road-widening. So to visit the less famous examples may be either an adventure or a disappointment. Nevertheless, when we visit a Celtic Cross we should do it with reverence, not in an offhand manner as just the next sight to 'do' on a jaded tourist trail. Crosses should be treated with respect, and we should always bear in mind that each Celtic Cross is sacred, bearing witness to the universal human recognition of the divine powers that lie beyond human understanding.

Brittany

Bazoges-la-Pérouse, Ile-et-Vilaine. La Pierre Longue (or La Pierre de Lande-Ros) stands near a stream between Bazoges and Noyal, 2 km (1 mile) from the crossroads of Trois-Croix. It is a megalith whose top has been carved into a cross.

Brigognan-Plage, Finistère. The Men Marz at the Terre-de-Point 1 km (about ½ mile) to the north-northwest of Brigognan-Plage is known as a miracle stone where St Pol de Leon stopped the encroachment of the sea. It bears a small cross on its summit.

Carnac-Ville, Carnac. La Pierre Chaude (or Cruz-Moquen) is a megalithic tomb upon which stands a tall stone cross.

Hameau de Rungleo, Finistère. Near Daoulas (45 km/28 miles southwest of Morlais, 18 km/11 miles eastsoutheast of Brest) is the Croix des Douze Apôtres, a megalith rededicated as a Christian monument in the late medieval period. The figures resemble those on the base of the cross at Moone, County Kildare, Ireland.

Kerégard-Vraz, Plumeur, Finistère. (23 km/14 miles southwest of Quimper, 6 km/3½ miles west of Pont l'Abbé.) Narrow, rounded, granite megalith cross.

Lanrivoaré, Finistère. Close to the church is 'The Moaning-Place', eight megalithic boulders, with a stone cross, that mark, it is said, a massacre in the fifth century.

Penvern, Côte-du-Nord. (9 km/5½ miles northwest of Lannion, 3 km/2 miles northnortheast of Trébeurden.) The cross of St Duzec, 8.1 m (26½ ft) high, is a megalith that was rededicated as a Christian monument in 1674. It bears carvings of the instruments of the passion, and has a cross bearing the crucified Christ on top. Also near Penvern, near Keralies, is one of St Samson's menhirs, next to a chapel constructed between 1575 and 1631.

Plévenon, Côte-du-Nord. At Cap Fréhel, 3 km (2 miles) northeast of Plévenon, is L'Aiguille de Gargantua, a megalith re-fashioned as a shaft surmounted by a cross.

St Samson-sur-Rance, La Tremblais, Côte-du-Nord. 5 km (3 miles) northeast of Dinan in the village of St Samson close to the road to La Quinardais is another of St Samson's stones with finely incised bands of rectangles with cupmarks.

Great Britain

Aberlemno, Tayside (NO 5255). Alongside the B9134 road in Aberlemno are three Pictish 'symbol stones', while the churchyard to the east of this road contains the misleadingly named 'Aberlemno Stone', an eighth-century stone with an incised cross accompanied by beasts and hunting scenes.

Babingley, Norfolk (TF 6726). The stump of a cross near the crossroads, Boteler's Cross, could be the site of the first Christian settlement in East Anglia, founded by St Felix of Burgundy in the seventh century.

Bangor, Gwynedd (SH 5872). The Museum of Welsh Antiquities at Bangor contains some early Celtic cross-slabs.

Beverley, Humberside (TA 0339). Three of the four crosses that marked the boundary of the sanctuary of Beverley Minster can be seen: at Walkington (TA 0037), the cross is a stump in the hedge at the beginning of the village; Stump Cross at Killingwoldgraves (TA 0039); and next to the Beverley-to-Hessle road at Bentley (TA 0236).

Borthwick Mains, Borders (NI 4314). A Pictish symbol stone, in the private garden of a farm 6.4 km (4 miles) west of Hawick, once stood in the River Teviot. Carved on the stone is a fish whose tail is said to be a marker of the level of water at which it was safe to ford the river.

Brechin, Tayside (NO 5960). Preserved in the cathedral is a fragment of cross that has an image of the Madonna and Child in a circular medallion at the centre of the cross-head. There is also the fine Celtic cross-slab called the Aldbar Stone. The front is carved with interlace while the rear has animals, humans and implements.

Brecon, Powys (SO 0428). Brecknock Museum on Captain's Walk in Brecon has a collection of stone stelae and crosses, including the Neuadd Siarman cross from Llanynys.

Bridell, Dyfed (SN 1742). In the churchyard stands a pointed megalith inscribed with an ogham text, which, translated, reads 'Nettasagrus, son of the descendant of Brecus'.

Carew, Dyfed (SN 0403). Beside the A4075 road, in the wall close to the castle entrance, is an eleventh-century cross, commemorating King Maredudd ap Edwin, who ruled Deheubarth (the kingdom of South-West Wales) from 1033 until 1035.

Cardinham, Cornwall (SX 1269). The church has a fine Celtic Cross of typically Cornish tradition.

Carmarthen Museum, Old Bishop's Palace, Abergwili, Carmarthen, Dyfed (SN 4120). This museum has a collection of early Christian monuments, including the stone of Voteporix Protector.

Carnoustie, Tayside Region (NO 5137). In the grounds of Panmure House, 6.5 km (4 miles) north of Carnoustie, stands the Camus Cross or Jesus Stone, a late Celtic Cross without a wheel-head.

Chapel of Garioch, Grampian Region (NJ 7124). A 3.6-metres (12-ft) high cross-shaft called 'The Maiden Stone' stands just outside the village.

Clackmannan, Central Region (NS 9191). In the churchyard is the phallic megalith that was used in the ceremony of inauguration by Pictish rulers. Next to it is a stepped perron.

Compton, Surrey (SU 9547). The Watts Mortuary Chapel at Compton is a remarkable symbolic building in Celtic Arts-and-Crafts style, designed by the Scottish artist Mary Fraser-Tytler Watts, constructed in 1896. Terracotta Celtic Cross motifs are used in the building and as tombstones in the graveyard.

Cringleford, Norfolk (TG 1905). Parts of a 'runic cross', discovered during rebuilding in 1898, are on the wall behind the font.

Dartmoor, Devon. The sacred stopping-places on the monastic trackway between Tavistock (SX 4774) and Buckfast (SX 7367) are marked by the following crosses: Tavistock Abbey – Green Lane Cross – Pixies' Cross – Warren's Cross – Huckworthy Cross – Walkhampton Church House Cross – Yannandon Cross – Lower Lowery Cross – Lowery Cross – Lether Tor Bridge – Clazywell Cross – Newleycombe Cross – Siward's Cross – Nun's Cross – Goldsmith's Cross – Childe's Tomb Cross – Mount Misery Cross – West Ter Hill Cross – East Ter Hill Cross – Skaur Ford Cross – Horse Ford Cross – Horn's Cross – Two Thorns Cross – Play Cross – Hawson Cross – Buckfast Abbey.

Dunfallandy, Tayside (NN 9456). Here is a Pictish cross-slab which shows the boss-style at its most prominent, and some of the finest beast-carvings on a Celtic Cross.

Dunning, southwest of Perth, Tayside (NO 0114). On the road to Milhaugh, west of Dunning, is a person-cross that stands upon a rough stepped-stone base. It is respected as the memorial to Maggie Wall, who was burnt there as a witch in 1657.

Dunkeld, Tayside (NO 0242). Preserved in the cathedral is the Apostles' Stone, a piece of cross-shaft with carvings of 12 figures, stylistically related to many 'Twelve Apostles' Stones' elsewhere.

Dupplin, near Forteviot, Tayside (NO 0518). An Irish-influenced free-standing cross is here.

Ewenni Priory Church, Glamorgan (SS 9177). This church has a number of interesting cross-slabs.

Forres, Grampian (NJ 0358). The tenth-century Sueno's Stone, over 6 m (20 ft) high, is carved with contemporary scenes of hunting and battle.

Fowey, Cornwall (SX 1152). On the A3082 near Fowey is the Tristan Stone, a pedestal bearing a sixth-century stone with an inscription commemorating Drustanus, perhaps the Arthurian Tristan or Tristram. Before 1971, the stone stood at the Four Turnings crossroads near Menabilly.

Fowlis Wester, Tayside region (NN 9223). The 'sculptured stone' of Foulis Wester is a fine cross-slab which depicts a free-standing wheel-head cross flanked by seated figures. The cross is ornamented with spirals, interlace and key-patterns.

Govan, Strathclyde (NS 5565). The old Govan church contains a collection of ancient Celtic Crosses and other worked stones.

Great Ashfield, Suffolk (TL 9968). A wheel-head cross stands in the grounds of Ashfield House. In former times, it was used as a bridge over the stream at the churchyard entrance.

Hackness, North Yorkshire (SE 9690). A fragment of eighth-century cross is kept in the church, which is the site of an Anglo-Saxon nunnery. Carved with interlace, it bears a multiple inscription in standard runes, the cryptic runes known as *hahalruna*, and ogham.

Hilton, Cambridgeshire (TL 2966). The parish church has a small but ancient Celtic Cross attached to the west wall.

Hoxne, Suffolk (TM 1876). In a field close to Hoxne is a cross on steps, erected in 1870 to commemorate the reputed execution of King Edmund of East Anglia on a tree that stood at this place until 1848.

Iona, Inner Hebrides, Strathclyde (NM 2726). The old Gaelic name for Iona is Innis na Druineach (The Isle of the Druids). St Columba founded St Mary's Abbey there in 563, and by the Reformation there were over 350 Celtic Crosses on the island. At the Reformation, Protestants threw over 200 of them into the sea, so now only the fifteenth-century Maclean's Cross and the tenth-century St Martin's Cross remain standing.

Kedington, Suffolk (TL 7047). On the gable at the east end of the church is the uppermost part of an ancient wheel-head cross, which was placed there after it was excavated from beneath the chancel floor.

Keills, Strathclyde (NR 6980). The old chapel here contains several Celtic crosses and other carved stones.

Kenidjack, Cornwall (SW 3631 and SW 3645). Two cross-pillars, from Trevorian in Sennen Parish, stand in the grounds of Boscean Hotel.

Kildalton, Islay (NR 4550). The tenth-century wheel-headed Celtic Cross in Kildalton churchyard is the finest in Scotland.

Kilmory, Knap, Strathclyde (NR 7075). At Kilmory is an old chapel containing Celtic Crosses and other Celtic carvings.

Lanherne, St Mawgan, Cornwall (SX 2368). A notable Cornish cross stands here.

Laugharne, Dyfed (SN 3011). A notable Celtic Cross is preserved at the church.

Littleton Drew, Wiltshire (ST 8280). Two cross-fragments at the church may be the remains of one of the crosses erected to mark a stopping-place of St Aldhelm's funeral procession from Doulting to Malmesbury.

Llandewibrefi, Dyfed (SN 6755). The parish church has a fine cross.

Llandough, South Glamorgan (SS 9972). The churchyard of St Dochdwy contains a unique four-section pillar cross, 'The Stone of Irbic'.

Llangammarch, Powys (SN 9347). Over the door of the church porch is a fragment of a ninth-or tenth-century sunwheel-cross, with a human figure and a spiral below, perhaps a serpent.

Llan-gan, West Glamorgan (SS 9678). A ninth-or tenth-century disc-headed sandstone cross bearing a figure of Christ stands in the churchyard.

Llangollen, Clwyd (SJ 2044). A stone cross-shaft known as 'The Pillar of Eliseg' is in a railing enclosure close to the Cistercian Abbey of Valle Crucis.

Llantwit Major, South Glamorgan (SS 9678). In the church is a rather poorly presented collection of ancient Celtic Crosses, including that of Hywel ap Rhys, king of Glywysing, who died in 886, and a remarkable serpent's head.

Lonan, near Ballamenaugh, Isle of Man (SC 4279). This has a notable cross-slab.

Ludgvan, Cornwall (SW 5033). The churchyard contains a cross-slab and two larger ancient standing crosses.

Margam Stones Museum, The Old School House, Margam, West Glamorgan (SS 7887). A valuable collection of ancient Celtic Crosses and slabs from the early days of the Christian religion in Wales. It includes the sixth-century Bodvocus stone. In the ninth and tenth centuries, there was a school of cross-sculptors at Margam, and the Conbelin wheel-head cross displayed here is a fine example of their work.

Maughold, Isle of Man (SC 4991). The churchyard has a collection of Celtic Crosses and stones.

Meigle, Alyth, Tayside (NO 2844). An important collection of Pictish cross-slabs is displayed here.

Merthyr Mawr, Mid Glamorgan (SS 8877). Here there is a panelled cross with a broken interlaced head, a characteristic example of the style.

Methwold, Norfolk (TL 7394). At Cross Hill is an ancient stone that once held a wooden cross-shaft, now lost.

Mold (Yr Wyddgrug), Clwyd (SL 2363). In Maesgarmon Field, off the Gwernaffield Road, stands the 'Alleluia Stone', erected by Nehemiah Griffith in 1736 to commemorate the victory of Bishop Germanus's army over Saxon and Pictish forces in the year 429.

Montrose, Tayside Region (NO 7157). Preserved in the museum at Montrose is the damaged Pictish cross-slab from Farnell, which has a famous image of the Tree of Life with Adam and Eve, two serpents and a cross.

Mylor, Cornwall (SW 8235). The churchyard contains the tallest cross in Cornwall, with solar carvings.

Nanquidno, Cornwall (SW 3629). A wheel-head cross, with a cross and bosses in relief, marks a stopping-place on the track to Nanquidno Farm.

Nevern, Dyfed (SN 0839). The churchyard contains a phallic stone and a Celtic Cross, dating from the tenth or eleventh centuries. Inside the church are ancient cross- and ogham-stones. At the end of the churchyard is the nineteenth-century Celtic Cross marking the grave of the bard Tegid, the Reverend John Jones.

Nigg, Highland (NH 8071). In the old parish church is the broken cross-slab notable for its fine bosses, carved with interlace and six-fold spirals.

Old Town, St Mary's, Isles of Scilly (SV 9210). A granite cross formerly at High Cross Lane, Salakee, is mounted on the gable end of St Mary's Church at Old Town.

Paul, Cornwall (SW 4627). On the churchyard wall is a four-hole wheel-head with a clothed Christ figure. Nearby is a round-headed cross, the shaft of which has carved crosses.

Penally, Dyfed (SS 1199). The church contains a whole wheel-head cross with interlace and scroll patterns, with some original red colour remaining, and a second fragment with opposed animals and interlace.

Pendrea, Cornwall (SW 4025). A round-headed cross with a cross on one side and Christ on the other stands by the road from Buryan to Land's End.

Penmon, Anglesey (SH 6380). The Priory Church contains two notable Celtic Crosses.

Penrith, Cumbria (NY 5130). In St Andrew's churchyard are cross-fragments that mark 'The Giant's Grave', said to be the grave of the giant Isir, who resided in a nearby cave.

Penzance, Cornwall (SW 4730). Outside the Penlee Museum, Morrab Road, Penzance, is preserved a notable tenth-century wheel-head cross which once stood at another site, serving as a market cross. Its shaft is divided into panels, some of which bear peck-marks that may have held painted cement or plaster in former times. There are the remains of an inscription, interpreted as *Regis Ricati Crux*, 'The cross of King Ricatus'.

Perranporth, Cornwall (SW 7756). A cross mentioned in a charter of the year 960 stands close to the celebrated 'lost church'.

Rosemorran, Cornwall (SW 4732). In the hedge at the back of the farmyard is a round-headed cross, which has Christ on one side and a cross on the other.

Rossie Priory, Tayside (NO 2930). The characteristic Pictish 'page in stone'.

Rudston, Yorkshire (TA 0967). At Rudston Church is a millstone grit pillar which is the largest megalith in a British churchyard.

St Buryan, Cornwall. Close to St Buryan are a number of interesting crosses. At Boskenna (SW 4324) on the B3315 to the southeast of St Buryan, is a broken, wheel-head cross set into a cider-press stone. Another is located to the north of it at Vellansagia (SW 4325), and to the northwest of St Buryan (SW 3927), next to a fine milestone, is Crows-an-Wra, 'The Cross of the Witch'.

St Cleer, north of Liskeard, Cornwall (SX 2468). Near the fifteenth-century house of St Cleer's Well is a Latin cross, while on the road to Redgate about 1.5 km (1 mile) away is the fragment of a tenth-century inscribed stone that recalls the memory of Doniert, King of Cornwall, who drowned in the River Fowey in 872.

St David's Dyfed (SM 7525). The chapel containing the relics of St David has an altar composed of a number of ancient Celtic cross-slabs and test-pieces.

St Dogmaels, Dyfed (SN 4715). In the abbey ruins is a lapidarium that contains many interesting old stones, including several cross-slabs, one of which is humanoid.

St Just, Cornwall (SW 3631). St Helen's Chapel at Cape Cornwall has an ancient cross erected on a gable end.

St Michael's Mount, Cornwall (SW 5129). This holy mountain of the Sun contains four crosses that mark sacred stopping-places around the former monastery.

St Vigeans, Tayside (NO 6342). At St Vigeans is an important collection of Pictish cross-slabs, one of which (The Drosten Stone, St Vigeans I) has a *sheela-na-gig*. On the back of this stone is the earliest known representation of a crossbowman.

Sancreed, southeast of St Just, Cornwall (SW 4129). Sancreed churchyard possesses two notable wheel-head monolithic crosses, one of which bears an image of the Christ and the inscription *Runho*, perhaps the crossmaster's name.

Southrepps, Norfolk (TG 2636). The broken shaft of an Anglian cross stands near the crossroads outside the village.

Temple, Cornwall (TX 5574). A number of ancient cross-incised stones and stone crosses are built into the wall of this church.

Terrington St John, Norfolk (TF 5415). The vicarage garden contains one of the crosses known as 'Hickathrift's Candlesticks'. It was named after the mythic giant of the Norfolk marshland, Tom Hickathrift.

Thurso, Highland region (ND 1168). Thurso Museum has a fine collection of Pictish stones, among them the eighth-century Ulbser and Skinner Stones, with crosses and beasts.

Tilney All Saints, Norfolk (TF 5618). Two crosses in the churchyard, called 'Tom Hichkathrift's Candlesticks'.

Towton, North Yorkshire (SE 4839). Next to the B1217 Towton Lane is Lord Dacre's Cross, erected to commemorate the battle fought there on Palm Sunday, 1461, in which 36,000 died.

Trelleck, Gwent (SO 5005). Outside the church is a stone cross, standing on a stepped 'world mountain' base, erected by an early medieval king of this part of Wales.

Walsingham, Norfolk (TF 9336). Some of the stopping-places of pilgrim routes to Walsingham, Britain's primary

Marian shrine, were marked by crosses, some of which still remain: e.g. at Binham (TG 9839); Caston (TG 9697); Gresham (TG 1838); Hemsby (TG 4917); and Weeting (TG 7739).

Whissonsett, Suffolk (TF 9123). The church contains the remains of a stone cross with interlace.

Whitecross, Cornwall (SW 5234). Beside the main A 30 road in Ludgvan parish stands a cross-head supported by two stone blocks. It is whitewashed annually in a ceremony.

Whitford, Clwyd (SJ 1477). Maen Achwyfan, 'The Stone of Lamentations' is a late tenth-century wheel-head cross-slab with designs related to Northumbrian cross-decoration, including spirals and interlace.

Whithorn, Galloway (NX 4440). The museum at Whithorn contains a collection of crosses.

Ireland

Ahenny, Kilkenny (X 2413). At the monastic settlement of Kilclispeen are two eighth-century high crosses. The North Cross, which is damaged, is a remarkable sunwheel with five prominent bosses, a finely carved wheel and a conical capstone.

Ardboe, Tyrone (H 2937). The high cross with Biblical figures is reputed to be the finest in the north of Ireland.

Boa Island, Lower Lough Erne, Fermanagh (G 2136). At the west end of the island, in the cemetery of Caldragh, stand a Pagan Janiform stone figure and another image called 'The Lusty Man'. Also, lined up in a roofless twelfth-century church, is a collection of seven stone figures dating from around 900. They include a *sheela-na-gig*, a seated man holding a book, and an ecclesiastical figure with crozier and bell.

Cardonagh, Inishowen, Donegal (C 2444). West of Cardonagh is the Donagh Cross or St Patrick's Cross. It is said to be the oldest low-relief cross still standing in Ireland.

Castledermot, Kildare (S 2818). Castledermot, named after St Diarmuid, the founder (*c.* 800), has two interesting high crosses, the north of which has particularly fine spiral carvings on its 'holy mountain' base.

Clones, Monaghan (N 2532). There is a Celtic Cross in the centre of the town of Clones.

Clonmacnois, Offaly (N 2023). This is one of the most important Celtic Church foundations in Ireland, founded by St Ciarán in 548 on royal ground given by King Diarmid. It has several fine Celtic high crosses and a remarkable collection of Celtic grave-slabs with crosses, interlace and inscriptions.

Cooley, Donegal (N 2544). In the cemetery of Cooley, 3 km (2 miles) north of Moville, the reputed burial place of St Finian, are two notable crosses.

Devenish, Fermanagh (H 2234). Daimh Inish, the Island of Oxen, in Lower Lough Erne, the holy island of St Molaise, has an unusual cross, as well as a monastic museum.

Durrow, south of Kilbeggan, Offaly (N 2323). Northeast of Durrow Abbey is a tenth-century high cross and the holy well of St Columba.

Dysert O'Dea (R 1218). The high cross here has interlace and zoomorphic figures, and a stone representing St Tola, the eighth-century founder.

Fahan, Buncrana, Donegal (C 2343). 7 km (4½ miles) south of Buncrana, at Fahan, is St Mura's Cross, a stone with remarkable interlace and human figures. Close by is another cross-slab built into a roadside wall.

Glen of Aherlow, Tipperary (R 1913). At Ardane, in the south of the Glen of Aherlow, is the oval sacred enclosure called St Berechert's Kyle, which has two ancient crosses and over 50 cross-slabs set on the drystone walls.

Glendalough, Dublin (T 3119). The Vale of Glendalough contains many sacred remains associated with the sixth-century monastic settlement of St Kevin. They include St Kevin's Cross (*c.* 1150).

Inishcealtra (Holy Island), in Lough Derg, Clare (R 1618). The holy island of St Caimin has a circular enclosure with the Cross of Cathasach (*c.* 1094).

Inishkeen, Upper Loch Erne, Fermanagh (H 2233). 5 km (3 miles) southeast of Enniskillen is Inishkeen, where St Fergus's cemetery contains an antlered stone head.

Inishtooskert, Blasket Islands, Kerry (Q 0210). This holy island has three stone crosses.

Kells (Ceanannas Mór), Meath (N 2727). In the market-place is a high cross on its original base. Among its carvings are several martial arts scenes, including quarterstaff fighting and wrestling. In the churchyard are crosses and a stone slab with an ancient sundial that shows the old northern European method of time-telling through the eight tides of the day. Close to the round tower is a high cross, with a Latin inscription, while next to the church is the unfinished cross that uniquely shows the stonemason's technique.

Kilfenora, Clare (R 1119). Here is an eleventh-century cross, which, with that at Dysert O'Dea (q.v.) is the most important example of the type in which a full-length figure of Christ is carved on the cross, transforming the Celtic Cross into a crucifix.

Killaloe, Limerick (R 1717). In the churchyard of St Flannan's Oratory is Thorgrim's Stone, dating from the first millennium, which is a cross-shaft inscribed in both the runic and ogham scripts.

Kilmakedar, Kerry (Q 0411). A remarkable sundial-cross stands close to the Romanesque church. It is in the form of a wheel-headed cross with a flattened top, resembling some of the carved crosses at Clonmacnois.

Kilnasaggart, Louth (O 3031). Here there is an inscribed granite pillar dating from around the year 700.

Loughrea, Galway (M 1622). 6.5 km (4 miles) northeast of Loughrea is the Turoe Stone, a phallic-shaped *omphalos* with La Tène-style carvings.

Monasterboice, Louth (O 3028). The Celtic monastery founded by St Buithe has three ancient crosses. Muiredach's Cross (*c.* 923) is one of the most finely developed and executed Celtic Crosses in existence. It has a crucifix-sunwheel with 'world mountain' base and 'heavenly house' capstone. The North and West crosses are also particularly note-worthy, as is the pillar sundial which is also carved with a wheel-cross.

Moone, Kildare (N 2719). The Moone Cross stands in the grounds of Moone Abbey. It is over 5 metres (16 ft) tall. Its base bears a crucifixion scene, while the sunwheel-head has a four-fold spiral pattern.

Nendrum, Down (J 3536). The tallest sundialpillar in Ireland stands in the churchyard here. Rediscovered as fragments in the 1920s, it was pieced together and re-erected.

Reask (Riasc), Kerry (Q 0310). The pillar-cross here is asymmetrically shaped, following the horizon, with the remains of a former drilled hole at the left.

St Mullins, Carlow (S 2713). 12 km (7½ miles) north of New Ross at the holy place of St Moling is a ninth-century high cross.

Stepaside, Dublin (O 3122). North of Stepaside Farm, below the Three Rocks Mountain, are Jamestown Holy Well and cross.

Tallaght, Dublin (O 3022). St Máel-Rúáin's Cross stands in the churchyard of St Maelruan's church.

Tara, Meath (N 2925). Tara of the Kings (Teamhair na Riogh), the ancient royal capital of Erin, has many features, including the pillar-stone called *Lia Fáil*, said to be the inauguration-stone of the High Kings of Ireland.

Tory Island, Donegal (B 1844). In the ruined monastery are many cross- and slab-fragments, including the famous cursing-stones.

Tuam, Galway (M 1425). This has a fine twelfth-century cross.

Tullylease, Cork (R 1311). The ruins of the monastery of Tullylease contain St Berechert's Well and the Berechtuine Stone, an eighth-century cross-slab sculpted with spiral and geometrical patterns.

Tynan, Armagh (H 2734). Tynan Abbey, west of Armagh, has four stone crosses, probably dating from the eighth century. The Village Cross and thc Terrace Cross were taken in 1844 from Egish churchyard, while the Well Cross and Island Cross were brought to Tynan from Glenarb.

White Island, Lower Lough Erne, Fermanagh (H 2135). The ruined church on White Island contains seven sculpted stone images of Pagan and Christian figures.

BIBLIOGRAPHY

Allen, J. Romilly and Anderson, Joseph *The Early Christian Monuments of Scotland*. Forfar, The Pinkfoot Press, 1993.

Anwyl, Edward *Celtic Religion*. London, Constable, 1906.

Bain, George *Celtic Art: The Methods of Construction*. Glasgow, McLellan, 1951.

Bamford, Christopher and Marsh, William Price *Celtic Christianity*. Edinburgh, Floris Books, 1986.

Bryce, Derek *Symbolism of the Celtic Cross*. Llandyssul, Gomer, 1989.

Chadwick, Nora K. *The Age of the Saints in the Early Celtic Church*. London, Oxford University Press, 1963.

Cubbon, M. *The Art of Manx Crosses*. Douglas, The Manx Museum and National Trust, 1971.

Davis, Courtney *The Art of Celtia*. London, Blandford, 1993.

de Paor, Máire and Liam *Early Christian Ireland*. London, Thames & Hudson, 1958.

Dillon, M. and Chadwick, N. K. *The Celtic Realms*. London, Cardinal, 1967.

Ellis-Davidson, H. R. *Myths and Symbols in Pagan Europe*. Manchester, Manchester University Press, 1988.

Evans-Wentz, W. Y. *The Fairy Faith in Celtic Countries*, Oxford University Press, 1911.

Gantz, J. *Early Irish Myths and Sagas* Penguin, 1981.

Green, M. J. *The Gods of the Celts*. Gloucester, Alan Sutton, 1986.

Grinsell, L. V. *Folklore of Prehistoric Sites in Britain*. Newton Abbot, David & Charles, 1976.

Hamlin, Ann *Historic Monuments of Northern Ireland*. Belfast, Department of the Environment, 1987.

Harbison, Peter *Pilgrimage in Ireland*. London, Barrie and Jenkins, 1991.

Hardings, Leslie *The Celtic Church in Britain*. London, 1972.
Henderson, Isabel *The Picts*. London, Thames & Hudson, 1967.
—*The Art and Function of Rosemarkie's Pictish Monuments*. Rosemarkie, 1991.
Henken, Elissa R. *Tradition of the Welsh Saints*. Cambridge, Cambridge University Press, 1987.
Henry, Françoise *Irish High Crosses*. Dublin, 1964.
Jones, David *Epoch and Artist*. London, Faber & Faber, 1959.
Jones, Prudence *Eight and Nine. Sacred numbers of Sun and Moon in the Pagan North*. Bar Hill, Fenris-Wolf, 1982.
—and Pennick, Nigel *A History of Pagan Europe*. London, Routledge, 1995.
Laing, Lloyd and Jennifer *A Guide to the Dark Age Remains in Britain*. London, Constable, 1979.
Mackey, James P. (ed.) *An Introduction to Celtic Christianity*. Edinburgh, 1989.
McNeill, F. Marian *Iona. A History of the Island*. Glasgow, 1920.
Megaw, Ruth and Megaw, Vincent *Celtic Art*. London, Thames and Hudson, 1990.
Merne, John G. *A Handbook of Celtic Ornament*. Dublin, Mercier Educational, 1974.
Michell, John *The Old Stones of Land's End*. London, Garnstone Press, 1974.
Okasha, Elisabeth *Corpus of Early Christian Inscribed Stones of South-West Britain*. Leicester, Leicester University Press, 1993.
Pennick, Nigel *The Ancient Science of Geomancy*. London, Thames and Hudson, 1979.
—*Einst War Uns Die Erde Heilig*. Waldeck-Dehringhausen, Felicitas-Hübner Verlag, 1987.
—*Celtic Art in the Northern Tradition*. Bar Hill, Nideck, 1992.
—*Anima Loci*. Bar Hill, Nideck, 1993.
—*The Oracle of Geomancy*. Chieveley, Capall Bann, 1995.
—*Secret Signs, Symbols and Sigils*, Chieveley, Capall Bann, 1996.

—*Celtic Sacred Landscapes*. London, Thames and Hudson, 1996.

Rees, Alwyn and Rees, Brinley *Celtic Heritage*. London, Thames & Hudson, 1967.

Richardson, Hilary and Scarry, John *An Introduction to Irish High Crosses*, Cork, Mercier, 1990.

Seaborne, Malcolm *Celtic Crosses of Britain and Ireland*. Aylesbury, Shire Archaeology, 1994.

Simpson, W. Douglas *The Ancient Stones of Scotland*. London, Hale, 1973.

Smyth, Alfred P. *Warlords and Holy Men*. Edinburgh, 1989.

Sutherland, Elizabeth *In Search of the Picts*. London, 1994.

Thomas, Charles *Christianity in Roman Britain to AD 500*. London, Thames & Hudson, 1981.

Thomas, Patrick *The Opened Door. A Celtic Spirituality*. Llandysul, Gomer, 1990.